'The heartfelt challenge in this
and consecrated, thus empowering

FORWARD BY DOUG STRINGER

Seven Women Shall Take Hold Of One Man

GOD'S INCREDIBLE PLAN OF
PROVISION, PROTECTION AND REVIVAL
FOR THE 21ST CENTURY CHURCH

JOHN LOUIS MURATORI
with Nick Gugliotti

Seven Women Shall Take Hold of One Man

ISBN: 0-9704753-0-6

Acknowledgments

First, I want to thank my Lord and Savior Jesus Christ for saving my soul and placing me in the Ministry. All the words of all the known languages could not express the sacrifice and price you paid for my soul. Serving you is my greatest honor and privilege.

To Carmela, my lovely wife and partner in life: Thank you for going through the valleys of life and ministry by my side. We have sowed in tears and we will reap in joy. Everything I accomplish is the result of our relationship to each other and to Jesus our Lord.

To my two sons John and Joshua: Thank you for allowing me to use our precious time together to write, Pastor, and travel. You are the best sons a father could ask for. Countless days of fishing and frog collecting are ahead of us.

To Nick Gugliotti: No one will ever know the travail and personal adversities we encountered birthing this book. It is difficult to express how much I value our friendship. Your desire to see the message of *"Seven Women"* in a book started this journey. To your lovely wife Dawn, thank you for releasing your husband to spend so much time with me.

To the Elders of Calvary Life: Thank you for hungering after Jesus and staying steadfast with your desire to see Revival visit New England. Your support for me as I sound this alarm throughout our Nation is noticed and treasured.

To Calvary Life and Turning Point: I am so blessed to Pastor such great and passionate ministries. Your compassion for the hurting, wounded and afflicted will continue to change our state, and hopefully help impact our culture and nation.

To my editor, Wallace Henley: You have no idea how blessed we are to have found you. Your gifting as an author, minister and editor made your contribution to this book invaluable.

Now, I do not really think anyone reads the acknowledgements except the people they were written too. With that in mind - many years ago I said I was going to thank all the people who said I would never succeed in anything. Those who said twenty years ago I was too young to preach. Those who used, abused, mistreated and talked about me over the years of ministry. The truth is, without your trial of my faith I would not be where I am today. Like Joseph, my response to your affliction helped shape my future. So in a strange way, "Thank you."

ENDORSEMENTS

John Muratori has written a powerful tour de force. *"Seven Women Shall Take Hold of One Man"* is a wake up call to all Christians. It is a prophetic pronouncement of how the church should prosper in the midst of poverty, be protected in an environment of lawless and go from its present day posture of pampering the proud to prophesying to the nations and preparing the humbled to lead. Muratori passionately identifies the problem and the needed answer for the Church and for America. Every maturity-seeking believer and leader must read this powerful and prophetic book.

—DR. JOHN P. KELLY
President, LEAD (Leadership Education for Apostolic Development)
Ambassador Apostle, ICA (International Coalition of Apostles)

John is one of the most innovative, entrepreneurial and bold young leaders emerging in the nation today. His concern for those in the church who reject the pure word of God and merely desire to use the name of Jesus as a front to cover or validate unbiblical lifestyles and attitudes is commendable. This book will definitely elicit a response in the reader; it will make a person mad or worse, glad. The Lord desires a repentance leading to intercession for some of the lukewarm social clubs impersonating the church in our present day.

—DR. JOSEPH G. MATTERA
Author, *"Ruling In The Gates"*
Pastor, Resurrection Church
Brooklyn, NY

Seven Women Shall Take Hold of One Man is a wake-up call for the 21st century church in need of reform. This book presents alarming statistical information gathered from many informed sources. The reader is forced to respond to these facts. The decisions made by its readers will shape the future course of the church worldwide. *Seven Women* is a must read for anyone interested in making an uncompromising commitment to live according to the truth of the word of God in a time of moral indifference and destruction.

—Apostle Joseph Kelley
Overseer, Building For Him Ministries

It's not often that we get to take a realistic look at ourselves. We want to look like we think others see us. Or we try to give the appearance that everything is just fine. When in truth, we are sick and need healing. John Muratori has, with grace, pulled the cover back enough for us to see the church as she really is. And he has received divine revelation on some of the most important steps to bring about her healing. This is not for the weak or faint hearted. This is for those who want to be His bride.

—Bishop Bart Pierce
Rock City Church, Baltimore, MD
Author, "Seeking our Brothers"

John Muratori is a husband, father, senior Pastor of a growing church, and Executive Director of Turning Point Christian Center, a national substance abuse rehabilitation program for men and women. He is passionate about the life-changing power of the Gospel of Jesus Christ. Through his study of the Word of God and pastoral experience, he firmly believes Jesus Christ is the only solution for the manifold problems in the world today. *"Seven Women Shall Take Hold of One Man"* is factual, forthright, topical, and challenging. It is my prayer that the Holy Spirit will use this book to inspire the Christian to zealously serve the Lord and convict the sinner to repent and accept Jesus Christ as Savior and Lord.

"For the time has come for judgment to begin at the house of God; and if it begins with us first, what will be the end of those who do not obey the Gospel of God? And if the righteous one is scarcely saved, where will the ungodly and the sinner appear? (1 Peter 4:17-18)

—Frank Butler
International Evangelist

CONTENTS

Introduction

I first heard *Seven Women Shall Take Hold of One Man* on a cool Sunday morning in September. I am used to Pastor John Muratori blowing people away with his grasp of scripture and his ability to communicate. In fact, I believe he is one of the finest preachers of our day—and that includes individuals with national and international ministries.

On this particular Sunday, he was at his best. What he pulled out of Isaiah chapter four is nothing short of inspired. The proof came in the next few days. People called to tell us of husbands repenting to their wives, relationships being restored and fathers and daughters reconciling. And all through the church everyone wanted more.

They simply could not let it go!

I knew, as did others in the church, that this message needed to go beyond the four walls of Calvary Life Christian Center. So I approached Pastor John with the idea of collaborating to write this book. It's not something he couldn't do on his own, but the man is a human tornado. He preaches, teaches, conducts leadership conferences, runs a growing church, runs a nationally recognized in-patient drug and alcohol rehabilitation program, heads an accredited Bible school and on and on. He agreed and we set to work.

What you hold in your hands is the result of many hours of work—filling in, adding, refining and developing that powerful message. There were moments throughout the writing of this book, when nothing short of *holy inspiration* took over. On many occasions we thought we were finished with a section, only to come back to it with new insight. I believe this book was written under the covering of the manifest presence of God.

There is certainly no lack of books to read. Yet, every now and then a book taps into exceptionally relevant information that intersects with the precise time it can do the most good. I believe *Seven Women* is that kind of book. There are some parts of the book that may *ruffle a few feathers*, but Pastor John's message was uncompromising and so the book must be the same. His conviction that this book would be "God-send" to those who are genuinely seeking a deeper relationship with God outweighs his concern about being disliked by some. A few times, while we were writing, I asked him, "Are you sure you want to say that?" To which his reply was always the same. "Is it the truth? Will it help readers understand what God is saying through the prophet Isaiah? Will it help people see the need for revival and a deeper passion for God?" Since the answer was always "Yes" the book you hold in your hand is not a watered down attempt to please everyone. Instead it is the heartfelt word of the Lord—delivered through one of the next generation of leaders being raised up by God.

You can read this book in several days. However, if you take your time and study the content, it will become a life-changing reference. *Seven Women Shall Take Hold of One Man* contains information you will not find anywhere else. It's a prophetic guidebook for the 21st Century church.

Nick Gugliotti
Oakville, CT

Foreword

In today's global and societal upheavals, and a world of such complexity and challenges, we need the unshakable and sure foundations of faith. Thus, we are in desperate need of those champions of faith who are willing to be courageous leaders of change. Those who can provoke us to think beyond the status quo of cosmetic Christianity, directing us in renewed vision and hope. John Muratori is one of those champions.

He is not merely presenting a list of theoretical concepts, but by the fruit of his life and ministry has proven to be a change agent and respected ambassador for Christ. He has a grasp and understanding of the times in which we live, recognizing the spiritual battles many face in the midst of the storms of life. We live in a world of spiritual cultural clashes battling for the very moral soul of a generation. Excellence is at war with mediocrity, righteous passion is being robbed by lethargy and apathy, and in the name of relevance we are willing to compromise our convictions. Genuine passion for God allows no room for compromise or mediocrity.

John R. Mott, a Nobel Peace Prize recipient in 1946 said, "Evangelism without Social Work is deficient, but Social Work without Evangelism is Impotent." Today when many are willing to compromise their convictions for a social gospel, and others are satisfied to proclaim a gospel without tangibility, we can be encouraged by the fact that there are those who rise above the crowd—who by their very lives provoke us to greater things. John Muratori and the ministries connected to him have become a prophetic conscience to us all. Fame can come in a moment, but greatness comes with longevity. As you read the heartfelt challenge in the pages of this book, you will find that it will deepen your resolve to live holy and consecrated, thus empowering you to be a living testament of change. Determine to draw from the life of this practitioner of prayer, compassion and evangelism. Determine to have your expectation in God raised, your call to consecration deepened, thus being wholly surrendered to God's divine purposes and plans for your own life and ministry.

Dr. Doug Stringer,
Founder- Somebody Cares America/International
& Turning Point Ministries International

We presently live on the threshold of great change—the final years, days, and hours before our Lord's Second Coming. Most of you are already aware of this. Though Jesus said we would not know the day or hour, He promised we would know the season—and it is upon us! Never before has such concurrent prophetic fulfillment occurred in the church, Israel, and nature.

—John Bevere
THUS SAITH THE LORD

Asleep in the Light

The world is sleeping in dark,
That the church can't fight, cause it's asleep in the light,
How can you be so dead, when you've been so well fed,
Jesus rose from the grave, and you, you can't even get out of bed.
How can you be so numb, not to care if they come,
You close your eyes and pretend the job's done,
Don't close your eyes, don't pretend the job's done.
Come away, from this mess, come away with Me, My love.

—Keith Green

ISAIAH

CHAPTER 4

And in that day seven women shall take hold of one man, saying, we will eat our own bread, and wear our own apparel: Only let us be called by thy name, to take away our reproach. In that day shall the branch of the LORD be beautiful and glorious, and the fruit of the earth shall be excellent and comely for them that are escaped of Israel. And it shall come to pass, that he that is left in Zion, and he that remaineth in Jerusalem, shall be called holy, even every one that is written among the living in Jerusalem: When the Lord shall have washed away the filth of the daughters of Zion, and shall have purged the blood of Jerusalem from the midst thereof by the spirit of judgment, and by the spirit of burning. And the LORD will create upon every dwelling place of mount Zion, and upon her assemblies, a cloud and smoke by day, and the shining of a flaming fire by night: for upon all the glory shall be a defense. And there shall be a tabernacle for a shadow in the daytime from the heat, and for a place of refuge, and for a covert from storm and from rain.

~1~

Cultural & Spiritual Chaos

Surely the Lord GOD will do NOTHING,
but He revealeth his secret unto his servants the prophets.

—Amos 3:7

Cultural & Spiritual Chaos

Surely the Lord GOD will do NOTHING,
but He revealeth his secret unto his servants the prophets.

—Amos 3:7

Cultural Chaos

"Where will the Church be in five to ten years and what will our communities look like?" I wrestle a lot with that question, among others.

America is swimming in lawlessness and wickedness. With just a simple glance, you will notice that Porn shops are everywhere. Prostitution, drug addiction, and violent crimes have infected every facet of our society. Gambling, once frowned upon, and illegal in many states, is becoming one of the fastest growing revenue streams nationwide through state lotteries and casinos.

We as a nation consume more prescription drugs than all other nations combined. We have created a pill for every problem. We have become so sedated that we are numb to the problems plaguing our country. Drunkenness, including closet alcoholism, is wreaking havoc in many families. What was considered to be strictly an inner-city problem has now made its way into the most affluent communities. Divorce, which is at an all time high, is being fueled by shows like "Desperate Housewives" and "Wife Swap."

Satan has made a mockery of Christian ethical values like honesty and integrity. He leads the attack on Godly covenants like marriage and family values. Christian free speech and the right to assemble are on the chopping block at the federal level.

Our generation is being indoctrinated with Witchcraft, Wicca, sorcery, and fortune telling. We see the acceptance and idolization of these things on shows like "Charmed," "Medium" and "Crossing Over"—where John Edwards purportedly speaks to the dead. Harry Potter books have sold more than 100 million copies in 40 languages globally. These books are nothing less than witchcraft manuals for innocent children. They expose and instruct children how to cast spells and curses, use black magic, enter into meditation, divination and sorcery, and commune with the dead. The prophet Daniel predicted these things.

"In the absence of light, darkness prevails."

> And through his (satan) policy also he shall cause craft (witchcraft and spiritism) to prosper …Dan. 8:25

Spiritual Chaos

In the two decades I have been in ministry, I have often cried out to God, "How can things continually get worse?" Only to hear heaven respond, "in the absence of light, darkness prevails." Even the church is not immune, as its sins continue to mount. Crooked evangelists are the least of our problems. The divorce rate in the church has risen to an astounding 67%—a number higher than that among non-believing couples. Youth groups across America face drug addiction, sexual experimentation, teenage pregnancies, and sexually transmitted diseases. Youth pastors are combating practices such as "friends with benefits.[1]" Christian homes, once marked by prayer and devotion, have become battle zones of strife and contention, resulting in broken relationships, disappointment, confusion and hurt.

All across America organized Christianity—including Catholics, Protestants, Charismatics, Pentecostals and mainline denominations—are wrestling with core beliefs never in question for 1,900 years of church history. Mainline denominations are splitting over the issue of homosexuality. Some have even ordained homosexuals as bishops and ministers. This may read as antiquated and outdated and maybe even homophobic, though I fall into none of those categories. I tend to be more "*Theo-phobic.*"[2] Nothing scares me more than bad theology and corrupt Christianity.

Nothing scares me more than bad theology and corrupt Christianity.

To the diligent Bible reader this should come as no surprise since scripture clearly predicts that these things would come to pass.

"In That Day..."

Throughout scripture, from the Old Testament to the New Testament, God has given us numerous[3] prophetic verses so we would know and understand the timetable of the Lord. I refer to these as "destination markers." For example, "*unto us a child is born*" (Isaiah 6) is clearly a messianic scripture. It was intended for the Jewish people so they would not miss Messiah. When the Pharisees came to Jesus asking for a sign as proof of his claims, without hesitation his rebuke to them was that they did not understand the signs of the times, or how God works in the affairs of men. He said:

> When evening comes, you say, 'It will be fair weather, for the sky is red,' and in the morning, 'Today it will be stormy, for the sky is red and overcast.' You know how to interpret the appearance of the sky, but you cannot interpret the signs of the times.
>
> —Matthew 16: 2,3 (NIV)

Note that the Bible clearly predicted His birth, life, ministry, death and resurrection. Actually, the casual student of the Word should have been able to match these prophecies to Jesus Christ, and without doubt declare he is the Messiah—the Son of God.

Another clear destination marker in scripture references the time of the second coming of Jesus. Specifically, the season that marks the close of the age of grace and the beginning of the tribulation period—also known as the "time of sorrows." The Bible refers to this period as "***that day***", "***the latter days,***" and "***the day of the Lord.***"

We want to be sure that in our generation we do not fall into the same trap—missing Christ once again. Beloved, let us heed the instruction of the Apostle Paul and…

> …study to show thyself approved unto God, a student that needeth not to be ashamed, rightly dividing the word of truth.
>
> —2 Tim. 2:15

Prophetic Headlines

The cultural and spiritual atmosphere of our time is found in these prophetic verses of scripture. This prophecy given by Paul to Timothy concerning the last days is so accurate it's as if he watched the evening news or had a copy of the daily newspaper.

> This know also, that in the "***Last Days***" perilous times shall come. For men shall be lovers of their own selves, covetous, boasters, proud, blasphemers, disobedient to parents, unthankful, unholy, without natural affection, trucebreakers, false accusers, lacking self-control, angry, despisers of those that are good, traitors, heady, conceited, lovers of pleasures more than lovers of God; Having a form of godliness, but denying the power thereof: ***from such turn away.***
>
> —2 Tim. 3:1-5

Paul wrote these prophetic verses while he was in prison. During this time in Paul's life, he witnessed confessing believers removed from their homes, imprisoned, beaten, stoned and beheaded for their faith. Yet, as he sees the depth of this prophecy and peers into a future day, he considers the times to come (***last days***) more perilous and dangerous. A closer look at this prophecy reveals the downward spiral of our present-day culture.

A closer look at this prophecy reveals the downward spiral of our present-day culture.

- For instance, this prophecy declares that "*men will be lovers of their own selves...*" We have never seen so many self-centered individuals, sacrificing and abandoning their families to fulfill their own self-centered desires in life.

- Further, Paul writes, individuals will be "*disobedient to parents...*" Teenage rebellion, once a "phase," is now a lifestyle as the spirit of rebellion sweeps across our country.
- People, says Paul, will be "*unthankful...*" The spirit of ingratitude affects all levels of society. Welfare, for example, created by government to assist needy individuals and families through difficult times, is now viewed by many as an entitlement.
- Paul continues that the day will come when some individuals will be *"without natural affection..."* There are innate natural instincts and behaviors placed in us by God, separating humans from animals. Paul was troubled by the beastly, unnatural and barbaric nature of man prophesied for the last days. So a young girl attends her prom, gives birth to her baby, drowns it in the toilet, dumps the body in the garbage and dances the last dance without remorse. There is also in our time the increase of mothers murdering their children through abortion. Beloved, without doubt, this is a clear prophetic picture of the days in which we live.

Paul is not the only writer who saw the coming of the last days. The prophet Daniel penned two full chapters dealing with the subject. Joel writes prophetically about it as well as others. One prophet who spoke with chilling accuracy is the prophet Isaiah.

Isaiah begins by setting a destination marker for his readers.

Isaiah presents one of the clearest prophecies about how the church and our culture will look just prior to the second coming of the Lord Jesus. As this book unfolds, I believe you will see a startling revelation about the culture we live in and the church of our day. You will also be able to examine yourself to be sure you are included under the Lord's protection and guidance for the perilous times that lie before us.

The first verse of chapter four reads, *"In that day, seven women shall take hold of one man."* Isaiah begins by setting a destination marker for his readers. Again, when Isaiah refers to "*that day*" he is not referring to his days but rather the "*last days.*" Like the previous prophets, he is also referring to the cultural and spiritual chaos prevalent in our day.

The majority of commentators and theologians dismiss this chapter as having very little prophetic implication. By missing the destination marker of "*that day*" you would be forced to interpret the verse as relevant only to Isaiah's time.

Beloved, this would be a TRAGIC OVERSIGHT!

2

Seven Women...One Man

*...come hither, I will shew thee the **bride, the Lamb's wife.***

Revelation 21:9

Seven Women...One Man

...come hither, I will shew thee the ***bride, the Lamb's wife.***

Revelation 21:9

Have you ever read a verse of Scripture that seems to make no sense and appears to have no significance? Usually, they are overlooked or misunderstood. For instance, in 1st Samuel the Bible reports that a man had six fingers and six toes, twenty four in all[1]. Why is this information recorded in the Bible? What could it possibly mean? You will stumble across other such seemingly nonsensical passages in the Bible. I'm sure you too have come across such verses.

Like the ***six fingers, six toes*** scripture, Isaiah four begins with an obscure reference to a time when ***"seven women shall take hold of one man."*** The majority of commentators overlook this chapter as if it is completely insignificant. Those who attempt an interpretation generally suggest the reference to "***seven women shall take hold of one man***" occurred during the reign of King Ahaz. At that time, enemy armies came against Ahaz and slew 120,000 men. While this is a historical fact, they make an assumption that the absence of 120,000 men caused seven women to take hold of or claim one man. Not only is this speculation, but also it does not address nor fit the subsequent events of Isaiah four. There is no evidence that this verse was fulfilled in the time of Ahaz or any other time in history.

There is also no evidence that this chapter has to do with the absence of a group of men. There is nothing to suggest that, even in Ahaz' time, seven women literally "took hold of one man."

Setting a Destination Marker

If this verse was not fulfilled in Ahaz' time, nor placed at any other historic period, who are these seven women and who is the one man of whom they desire to take hold? Isaiah clearly defines the time in which seven women shall take hold of one man. Twice in chapter four he states this will occur in *"that day,"* again referring to the time just prior to the second coming of Jesus Christ.

Throughout scripture, ***"that day"*** gives prophetic insight into four specific groups and their relationship to Jesus Christ. The four groups are Israel, the church, the culture, and Satan's kingdom.

The Bride of Christ

Jesus came to get Himself a bride.

Jesus not only provided access for salvation through His sacrifice on the cross, but also came to get Himself a bride. This reference of the church as the Bride of Christ is seen undeniably throughout the Gospels, the Epistles and the Book of Revelation. Scripture clearly defines the church as betrothed, engaged, and espoused to Christ.

Paul, writing to the Corinthian church, says...

> For I am jealous over you with godly jealousy: for I have espoused you to one husband (Christ) that I may present you as a chaste virgin to Christ.
>
> —2 Corinthians 11:2

Jesus refers to His Bride numerous times in the gospels. One reference is the parable of the ten virgins (Matthew 25). As they are waiting for the groom, five engage in foolish activities, causing them to miss his coming. The other five are called wise because they remain steadfast and watchful. They long for the coming of the groom.

Not only was Jesus excited about his wedding, but in the parable of the Marriage Supper His Father underwrites the ceremony, furnishes the banquet hall and garnishes the tables. Their expectation is that the event will be overflowing with guests (Matthew 22:1-10). This marriage between Christ and His church even has a best man.

> He that hath the bride is the bridegroom: but the friend of the bridegroom (John the Baptist), which standeth and heareth him, rejoiceth greatly because of the bridegroom's voice: this my joy therefore is fulfilled.
>
> —John 3:29

The Mystery of the Church

In Ephesians, Paul challenges husbands to love their wives through the example set by Jesus, who so loved His bride that He gave His life for her. The revelation contained in the 5th chapter of the book of Ephesians is considered by Paul to be a great mystery.

> For the husband is the head of the wife, even as ***Christ is the head of the church***: and he is the ***savior*** of the

> body (Church). Therefore as the church (Bride) is subject unto Christ, so let the wives be to their own husbands in every thing. Husbands, love your wives, even as Christ also loved the church (Bride), and gave himself for it; That he might sanctify and cleanse it with the washing of water by the word, That he might present it to himself a glorious church (Bride), not having spot, or wrinkle, or any such thing; but that it should be holy and without blemish. So ought men to love their wives as their own bodies. He that loveth his wife loveth himself. For no man ever yet hated his own flesh; but nourisheth and cherisheth it, even as the Lord the church (Bride): For we are members of his body, of his flesh, and of his bones. For this cause shall a man leave his father and mother, and shall be joined unto his wife, and they two shall be one flesh. ***This is a great mystery: but I speak concerning Christ and the church*** (Bride).
>
> —Ephesians 5 23-32, EMPHASIS ADDED

The seven women of Isaiah's prophecy are none other than the bride of Christ—the church. Now you may be wondering how seven women can represent one bride. Yet, Jesus does just that in the first four chapters of the Book of Revelation. He addresses His Bride through seven letters to seven churches.

The seven women of Isaiah's prophecy are none other than the bride of Christ—the church.

By addressing the church as seven distinct congregations Jesus is shedding more light on the secret Paul refers to as "the mystery of the bride of Christ." Jesus is also connecting these seven churches to the seven women of Isaiah's prophecy. It becomes more evident that these seven women are the seven churches in the book of Revelation when you look at the description of the "one man" they take hold of.

The One Man

In the second verse of Isaiah chapter four there is yet another prophetic destination marker beginning with the phrase "*in that day.*" The remaining part of the verse describes the *one man* as the ***Branch*** of the Lord.

> In that day shall the ***Branch*** of the LORD be beautiful and glorious…
>
> —Isaiah 4:2 EMPHASIS ADDED

Without question this is a direct Messianic reference to Jesus. The prophet Jeremiah spoke of the "Branch of the Lord" as well.

> Behold, the days come, saith the LORD, that I will raise unto David a righteous ***Branch,*** and a King shall reign and prosper, and shall execute judgment and justice in the earth.
>
> —Jeremiah 23:5 EMPHASIS ADDED

> In those days, and at that time, will I cause the ***Branch*** of righteousness to grow up unto David; and he shall execute judgment and righteousness in the land.
>
> —Jeremiah 33:15 EMPHASIS ADDED

Zechariah 3:8 reads: … for, behold, I will bring forth my servant the ***Branch.*** EMPHASIS ADDED

The one man is none other than JESUS CHRIST!

The genealogy of Christ is so important it is recorded in two Gospels—Matthew and Luke. Throughout the Old Testament it was an honor to be engrafted into the royal lineage that would bring forth Christ. Prophesies concerning that lineage reference the coming Messiah through various names and titles. Two of which are the ***Branch*** and the "Son of David".

> And there shall come forth a rod out of the stem of Jesse, and a ***Branch*** shall grow out of his roots...
>
> —Isaiah 11:1 EMPHASIS ADDED

Beloved, the seven women represent the present day church which is laying hold of the ***one man***—who is none other than **JESUS CHRIST!**

~3~

"We'll Eat Our Own Bread and Wear Our Own Apparel"

This people draweth nigh unto me with their mouth,
and honoureth me with their lips; but their heart is far from me.

—Matthew 15:8

...we will eat our own bread and wear our own apparel:
only let us be called by thy name, to take away our reproach.

—Isaiah 4:1

"We'll Eat Our Own Bread and Wear Our Own Apparel"

This people draweth nigh unto me with their mouth,
and honoureth me with their lips; but their heart is far from me.

—Matthew 15:8

...we will eat our own bread and wear our own apparel:
only let us be called by thy name, to take away our reproach.

—Isaiah 4:1

These seven women have an agenda and a purpose for taking hold of this one man. At first glance, this might appear to be a good arrangement *for Him,* since they have no desire that He provide food or apparel.

"Take hold" implies to seize with force or to grasp with self-centered motives and intentions. So what do these women want to take hold of? They are laying hold of this man because in His name lies the power to remove their reproach. The women are not looking for their sin to be removed, but the guilt, shame and reproach of their sinful lifestyles to be erased. This reproach is like a plague that can eat away at the core of a person's being.

For instance, after David sinned, he cried out to God:

> **Reproach** hath broken my heart; and I am full of **heaviness**: and I looked *for some* to take pity, but *there was* none; and for comforters, but I found none.
>
> —Psalm 69:20 EMPHASIS ADDED

The reproach David was experiencing was consuming every area of his life.

> And hide not thy face from thy servant; for I am in **trouble**: hear me speedily. Draw nigh unto my **soul**, *and* redeem it: deliver me because of mine enemies. Thou hast known my **reproach**, and my **shame**, and my **dishonor**...
>
> —Psalm 69:17-19 EMPHASIS ADDED

Sin will always produce disgrace, shame and dishonor.

Whether you are a born-again believer or a hardened sinner, with no concern for God, sin will always produce the **disgrace**, **shame** and **dishonor** known as reproach. King Solomon said:

> ...sin is a reproach to any people.
>
> —Proverbs 14:34

The women in Isaiah's prophecy want to be called by His name in order to have their reproach taken away. They are looking for the benefits of laying hold of Christ, but not the challenge to change and pursue holiness. What the seven women are saying is—*we want "forgiveness only" but not holiness, we want your name but we don't want to partake of you, we will lay hold of you but don't you lay hold of us.*

The Present Day Church

Isaiah is giving us a clear and accurate depiction of the present day church. We are witnessing what is considered by many to be the era of the mega church. There are larger congregations today than ever before in church history. These churches are filled with thousands of attendees. But a closer look at this phenomenon only uncovers the fact that the number of truly devoted believers is far smaller than the statistics would indicate.

Isaiah is giving us a clear and accurate depiction of the present day church.

The consistent message from their pulpits to attendees, radio and television audiences, and readers of their books is *"God loves you just the way you are. You're okay, I'm okay. He wants you to be a champion and a victor. Don't worry yourself—you're forgiven."* In these congregations sinners can regularly hear messages that will assist them in the removal of their reproach. Yet, they will never deal with the issue of their sin. I am stunned at how many sinners come to church, not to change, **but to have their guilt removed from them!**

Many churches have replaced the word of God with ten-minute skits that produce no conviction and impart no Gospel power at all. The preaching of holiness is becoming scarce. The challenge to be separate from the world is missing. There's very little spoken about sanctification or dealing with our besetting sins. Today, the most popular messages are about self-help, guilt-free living, and positive thinking. People do not want to hear

Today, the most popular messages are about self-help, guilt-free living, and positive thinking.

what would be considered a "hard gospel" anymore. They just want to know how to cope with their troubles in the times in which they live.

I'm sad to say that churches modeled after the seven women in Isaiah chapter four have very little power. They can lead someone to repeat the sinner's prayer. But they do not complete the process of cleansing and renewing. True Christianity produces real change—called fruit. Paul warned us about this present day condition of the church saying...

True Christianity produces real change.

> For the time will come when they will not endure sound doctrine; but after their own lusts shall they heap to themselves teachers, having itching ears; (Ministers, Preachers and Pastors who tell the people what they want to hear) And they shall turn away their ears from the truth, and shall be turned unto fables.
>
> —2nd Timothy 4: 3-4

Holiness & Sanctification

People like the women described in Isaiah 4 will always find a preacher who will allow them to live in their sin. This may sound harsh. Some may consider such an idea to be pentecostalism, isolationism, legalism or some other *ism*. But none of those are the message of this book. What I'm referring to is clearly defined in Scripture as holiness and sanctification.

In times past this was not considered a hard gospel. It was the message of every great move of God, including the Reformation and the first and second Great Awakenings. It's the very same proclamation of Charles Finney, Jonathan Edwards, and D.L. Moody. This was the message of the Wesley brothers, William Booth and the Founding

Fathers of our nation. *It's the message that ignited people with a passion to lay hold of Christ and to have Christ lay hold of them.* And when preached today it will ignite in you a passion for Christ that will change our culture and reshape our nation!

It will ignite in you a passion for Christ.

We will Eat Our Own Bread

These seven women say to this one man "*we will eat our own bread. You do not need to provide bread for us because we are content to provide it for ourselves. We have food and nourishment from another source.*" In fact, they do not even desire to *sup with Him.* Yet, they look to Jesus to lay hold of Him so that His name may take away their reproach. They do not realize that they can only provide ***"counterfeit bread"*** for themselves. The Bible says this type of bread is "defiled."

> ...their sacrifices shall be unto them as the bread of mourners; all that eat thereof shall be polluted: for their bread for their soul shall not come into the house of the LORD.
>
> —Hosea 9:4

Again, these seven women are the seven churches of the book of Revelation. In addressing His bride, Jesus writes to the believers of Thyatira, challenging them to be overcomers that they may eat of His hidden manna—the bread of heaven.

> To him that overcometh I will give to him the ***hidden manna...***
>
> —Revelation 2:17 EMPHASIS ADDED

Jesus removes all doubt by declaring He is ***the bread*** spoken of in scripture.

> ... I am the ***bread of life***: he that cometh to me shall never hunger; and he that believeth on me shall never thirst.
>
> —John 6:35

Cotton Candy Church

This bread (Christ) is not appealing to these women, nor does it appeal any longer to churches across America. They say, "*We don't want the bread of separation, holiness, purity, and self-denial. We'll provide our own bread.*" Much of the church today prefers the bread of its own making because it is not as demanding. Such churches preach a message in which there is no reproof; no smiting conviction, no fire from heaven, and no purification. All across America, people are feeding on cotton candy and feel-good messages. Sadly, these places are packed with thousands upon thousands of individuals who come for a weekly dose of ice cream.

All across America, people are feeding on cotton candy and feel-good messages.

This food provides no nourishment or lasting satisfaction. Beloved, throughout the week the church can be found at the tables of this world. Like Eve, many churches have developed an appetite for the forbidden. This lack of heaven's bread is producing an epidemic of starvation. Christians can barely stay saved, let alone win the victory in their personal lives. As a pastor, I see believers struggling for years with the

This lack of heaven's bread is producing an epidemic of starvation.

same sins—anger, pornography, lust, lying, gambling, gossip and many other sinful behaviors.

Many who *profess* Christ, are actually filled with themselves. They are critical about the things of God and cynical about people who are hungry for Jesus. They are prideful and haughty—able to see the splinter in someone else's eyes, but unable to see the beam in their own. This is the result of malnutrition, caused by feeding on everything but Christ.

The prophet Amos saw the famine of this day even more clearly than the prophet Isaiah. Amos prophesied that in the ***"last days"*** believers would be so accustomed to eating strange bread that Christ would remove himself from the menu, causing a famine of the "*Word of God.*"

> Behold, the days come, saith the Lord GOD, that I will send a famine in the land, not a famine of bread, nor a thirst for water (natural famine), but of hearing the words of the LORD: And they shall wander from sea to sea, and from the north even to the east, *they shall run to and fro to seek the word of the LORD*, and shall not find *it.*
>
> —Amos 8:11-12

As prophesied, today people are running from one conference to another, looking for the Word of the Lord. Even church growth statistics agree with the prophet Amos, showing that the expansion of churches is predominantly based on "transfer growth." People are running from one church to another. Today, more money is spent in churches keeping people saved than on saving new people.

Present-day believers have available countless books, 24-hour Christian radio and TV, along with a church on every corner. Yet, many grapple with spiritual immaturity.

Mega Problems

Look at the landscape of the church. With so many mega churches and available resources, we should be producing powerhouses for God. Believers should be coming out of their churches turning their cities upside down. Instead, much of the church is apostate, plagued with the same sins as our culture. Homosexuality in the pulpit, church splits and divisions, teenage pregnancies, adultery, divorce, child abuse, children out of wedlock …and the list goes on.

Beloved, there is supposed to be a difference between a believer's life and that of the non-believer. When people tell me they are saved, yet act as unbelievers, I must ask, "Saved from what?" Where's the fruit of their salvation?

We live in a time where Jesus stands at the doors of the church crying, "*if any man is thirsty and hungry let him come unto me.*"(John 7:37) After salvation, believers must come back to the table and begin to partake of His bread. Jesus, writing to the Laodicean church, stated that He was ***outside the church doors*** knocking, but no one would hear Him. The Laodicean church viewed itself as rich, increased with every good thing, and in ***need of nothing.*** Yet, Jesus viewed them as, "…wretched, miserable, poor, blind, and naked."

Today the church in America also thinks of itself as rich and in need of nothing. As the musicians play, the choirs sing and the preachers preach, Jesus says, *"Behold, I stand at the door, and knock: if any man hear my voice, and **open the door**, I will come in to him, and will sup with him, and he with me"* (Revelation 3:20 EMPHASIS ADDED).

Are you hungry for more of Jesus?

Beloved, do not be satisfied with just the removal of your reproach.

Resist the temptation to provide your own food. I challenge you to come out of your comfort zone and begin to cultivate an appetite and a hunger for the bread of heaven.

Are you HUNGRY for MORE OF JESUS?

We Will Wear Our Own Apparel

Further, these seven women have no desire or need to be clothed with the apparel of this man's house. They will provide for themselves clothes that suit their own tastes. They have no desire to be fashioned or fitted with the clothes He has laid out for them.

This is not the only place in the Bible where individuals sought to provide their own apparel. Clothes as we know them had their origin in the Garden of Eden (Genesis 2:25). As we first find Adam and Eve, they are naked. This man and woman carry on their daily routine in this manner for what could have been a very long time, never experiencing the embarrassment or shame that usually accompanies nakedness.

How could that be? Consider this, while Adam was naked in his humanity he was still clothed in innocence. Innocence was the original garment provided in the garden. The garment of innocence is still the cloak that covers every newborn baby. What person would consider an unclothed newborn shameful? That cloak of innocence seems to stay on children all the way through their infant years. In fact, I remember my sons stripping off their towels after being bathed, and running through the house with joy and laughter—never thinking their nakedness was in any way inappropriate.

Innocence was the original garment provided in the garden.

Adam and Eve's nakedness produced

no shame until the day they ate the forbidden fruit provided by the serpent (Genesis 3:7). This was not the provision of food abundantly supplied by God. This sin ripped the clothes of innocence off them both—leaving them exposed and naked. Now, in this new state, Adam immediately looked to provide himself adequate covering. He sowed fig leaves together for himself and Eve, thinking this would be sufficient.

Sin ripped the clothes of innocence from them.

The fact is nothing Adam could have fashioned would have solved this problem. Adam did not realize that his outward nakedness was only a reflection of a more serious and deadly inward condition. Adam's act of disobedience allowed sin to be engrafted into humanity. Sin was now a part of the DNA of mankind and would be passed down from generation to generation, meaning that every child born is born in sin—and no fig leaf will do. Scriptures inform us,

> Nevertheless, death reigned from Adam to Moses, even over them that had not sinned after the similitude of Adam's transgression, who is the figure of him that was to come.
>
> —Romans 5:14

> For as in Adam all die…
>
> —1 Corinthians 15:22

Adam's transgression placed the garment of innocence out of reach. Because justice must be served, God had one of two choices: either put Adam to death, or find a substitute willing to pay the penalty for his sin (John 3:16, 1 John 4:10). Romans 6:23 states that *the wages of sin is death.*

So it is, Christ sacrificed His innocence to pay for the penalty of our sin. This now makes available, once again, a robe of righteousness. Christ provided apparel suitable for Adam and mankind to walk in right standing with God.

Christ sacrificed His innocence to pay for the penalty of our sin.

These garments were also available for the seven women of Isaiah's prophecy, who chose instead to *wear their own apparel.* So it is with many believers today. They desire forgiveness and the removal of reproach but choose to wear the substitute garments abundantly available.

Worldly Garments

Every philosophy of enlightenment, self-help, humanism, socialism, Communism, Marxism, Fascism and the other *isms* of our world are nothing more than garments we fashion for ourselves to provide a covering for sin and nakedness. Religion, the most deceptive garment in Satan's collection, is fooling millions around the world by providing a false sense of righteousness.

Religion is the most deceptive garment in Satan's collection.

Satan knew he could not get rid of the garment of righteousness, so he created the largest garment industry humanity has ever seen. He fashions wardrobes of garments designed to give the impression that man can live in disobedience and still be covered. He has a garment for every sin imaginable.

Yet, none of those garments will provide adequate covering in the Day of Judgment, when we stand before God. Paul warns us that the robe of righteousness is not optional, but required apparel.

The robe of righteousness is not optional, but required apparel.

> ...that He might present to himself a bride, not having spot, or wrinkle, or any such thing; but that she should be holy and without blemish.
>
> —Ephesians 5:27

I pray you see the importance of being clothed with this garment and walking in purity. In fact, ***I suggest you read this chapter once a month,*** to remind you of the importance of the power of purity. Isaiah delighted in righteousness, purity and holiness saying,

> I will greatly rejoice in the LORD, my soul shall be joyful in my God; for He hath clothed me with the garments of salvation, He hath covered me with the ***robe of righteousness....***
>
> —Isaiah 61:10 EMPHASIS ADDED

Beloved, I pray you would see the beauty and benefit of the purest of garments ever woven and made available to you. Oh, that we would long to be clothed in purity, holiness and righteousness! Throughout history, wherever the Gospel was preached with power, these garments were distributed to those who received Christ. Mary Magdalene was a prostitute until she met Christ. He not only healed her, but He also clothed her with righteousness. Heaven never viewed her the same again. For she was now *clothed in His righteousness.*

Oh, that we would long to be clothed in purity, holiness and righteousness!

> ..."though your sins be as scarlet, they will be ***white as snow***; though they be red like crimson, they shall be like wool."
>
> —Isaiah 1:18 EMPHASIS ADDED

> He that overcometh, the same shall be clothed in ***white raiment***; and I will not blot out his name out of the book of life, but I will confess his name before my Father, and before his angels.
>
> —Revelation 3:5 EMPHASIS ADDED

When revival fires burn brightest, sin is purified and garments are made *white as snow*. Righteousness and the power to live in purity are distributed in abundance for those who long for holiness.

4

The Branch of the Lord Shall Be Glorious

In those days, and at that time, will I cause
the Branch of righteousness to grow up unto David;
and he shall execute judgment and righteousness in the land.

—Jeremiah. 33:15

In that day shall the branch of the Lord be ***beautiful and glorious,***
and the fruit of the earth shall be excellent and comely f
or them that are escaped of Israel.

—Isaiah 4:2

The Branch of the Lord Shall Be Glorious

In those days, and at that time, will I cause the Branch of righteousness to grow up unto David; and he shall execute judgment and righteousness in the land.

—Jeremiah. 33:15

In that day shall the branch of the Lord be ***beautiful and glorious,*** *and the fruit of the earth shall be excellent and comely f or them that are escaped of Israel.*

—Isaiah 4:2

Isaiah's reference to "that day," once again points to the last days. He prophesies there will be those who will see the branch of the Lord (Jesus) as beautiful, glorious, comely and excellent.

Are You Appalled Yet?

However, it is apparent our culture does not see Christ as beautiful and glorious. In fact, across America Jesus is being removed from public view. And where He is not removed He is often trampled un-

"All that is needed for evil to prevail is for good men to do nothing."

der foot, blasphemed and ridiculed. We have witnessed MTV, Hollywood and even modern art depict Him as anything but beautiful. What passes for art is disgraceful—upside down crosses in urine (funded at taxpayer expense!), and movies like "The Last Temptation of Christ" are becoming more common. Yet a Ten Commandments monument is ordered out of a courthouse foyer because it may be offensive to a very small minority. Such actions should be offensive to every believer. As Edmund Burke said, *"All that is needed for evil to prevail is for good men to do nothing."* This goes on day after day, as churches do nothing, and say nothing. These are just a few of the indignant, appalling and blasphemous ways our glorious Lord and Savior is portrayed in our culture.

You may view these statements as shock tactics but let me say this; *"I have passed the point of shock years ago. I am appalled and broken hearted over the way my Lord is treated."* Today many opinion-molders in our nation raise their fist towards God demanding He ***get out.*** These things, done in the name of free speech, should outrage every believer. How could this happen in a country where 64 percent of the population declared itself Christian in the last presidential election?

"I am appalled and broken hearted over the way my Lord is treated."

It's because, like the seven women, churches today want to be called by His name for the removal of reproach yet they want to *eat their own bread and wear their own apparel.* They simply do not behold him as beautiful and excellent nor do they ***love his appearing***

(2 Timothy 4:8). In our day, churches have become focused on public acceptance, full of fame-seeking preachers, well-known book promoters and hired-gun motivational speakers. For many, fame, notoriety and popularity have taken the place of conviction and the defense of the gospel. Paul said…

> Am I now trying to win the approval of men, or of God? Or am I trying to please men? If I were still trying to please men, I would not be a servant of Christ.
>
> —Galatians 1:10 (NIV)

Fame, notoriety and popularity have taken the place of conviction and the defense of the gospel.

Popularity Syndrome

The truth is celebrity pastors ***say nothing*** that is too convicting because they are more concerned about making the bestseller lists and the front row at Barnes and Noble.

Jesus warned His disciples to ***beware of popularity.*** In fact, He told them the world and their culture would not accept them even as they did not Him (Luke 6:22).

But these ministers justify themselves by saying they are reaching a pocket of people the church does not normally impact. I say they are ***not*** making a distinction between what is holy and what is unholy. Under the auspices of their leadership and influence, they are actually directing Christians away from maturity and strength in the Lord. It is my belief that his very issue infuriates God. God put the blame for the apostasy of Ezekiel's day squarely on the shoulders of the shepherds—as I believe He does in ***OUR*** day! I recommend that you slowly read the complete context of the following verse. (*context:* Ezekiel 22: 23-31)

> Her priests do violence to my law and profane my holy things; they do not distinguish between the holy and the common; they **teach that there is no difference between the unclean and the clean**; and they shut their eyes to the keeping of my Sabbaths, so that I am profaned among them.
>
> —Ezekiel 22:26 (NIV) EMPHASIS ADDED

The amplified sheds more light on the severity of the issue.

> Her priests have done violence to My law and have profaned My holy things. **They have made no distinction between the sacred and the secular, neither have they taught people the difference between the unclean and the clean** and have hid their eyes from My Sabbaths, and I am profaned among them.
>
> —Ezekiel 22:26 (AMP) EMPHASIS ADDED

This type of leadership has cheapened and watered down the Gospel—rendering it powerless. We have lifted up the pulpit and the preacher rather than lifting up Christ. People stand in line for hours to get an autographed book from a preacher when they should be more concerned with the *book of life* authored by Jesus Christ and signed in His blood.

Making a stand for Christ is not always popular. Ministers and believers need to stop politicking and listening to popularity polls, fearful to ruffle any feathers.

Making a stand for Christ is not always popular.

The great revivalist John Wesley once got down from his horse and began to pray, asking God to show him if his lack of persecution was due to any un-confessed sin. While he was on his knees before God, an unsaved man passing by recognized him as the preacher he disliked. The man picked up a brick and tossed it at Wesley. It missed the evangelist, but John Wesley saw it as an answer to prayer. "Thank God," he exclaimed, "it's all right. I still have His presence."

Another writer of his day stated, "If one has not been persecuted for his Christian faith, he has not walked with Christ long enough or close enough.[1]"

I recently watched an interview on a national television news magazine with a high profile preacher who has sold millions of books, and is on the *New York Times* Best Seller List. The show began with a tour of his enormous church headquarters. During the one-on-one interview he was asked, "you have taken slack from other ministers because you will not speak against or speak about controversial issues such as abortion and homosexuality. Why don't you address these issues head on?" The preacher responded that indeed he *will not* speak about or refer to abortion as a sin because he did not want to alienate any woman in his audience who may have had an abortion. He doesn't want her to feel bad. Instead, he would rather share about the love of Jesus.

By ignoring the topic, is one really expressing the love of Jesus?

As I pondered the interview, I thought about what will happen to the multitude of women who are contemplating an abortion. Don't they need to know God's position on this issue? Don't they deserve to know the pain associated with the consequences of their choice? By ignoring the topic is one really expressing the love of Jesus? I think not!

This is not a gray area of scripture. Abortion is nothing less than murder. And murder should never be the choice of a woman over her unborn child. Likewise, in the Bible, homosexuality is not a debate. It is an abomination to God (Romans 1:27).

The Price of Mediocrity

As you read this, there is a militant homosexual movement waging an all-out attack on the Gospel of Jesus Christ and organized Christianity. They single out Christianity, because it is the ***only effective antidote*** to the homosexual lifestyle. While homosexual groups try to propagate false scientific data, such as the "discovery" of the gay gene, the power of the Gospel, through Jesus Christ, is liberating thousands of homosexuals. Every time a homosexual is set free from the sin of homosexuality, *it proves the lifestyle is a choice.* The fact is people are not created homosexual, they ***choose*** to be.

Christ has made available the cloak of righteousness.

The Gospel dispels the myth that God created homosexuals this way. If homosexuals are successful in their lobbying effort, they will categorize preaching against the sin of homosexuality as a hate crime, bringing automatic jail time. There may come a day when my written and published opinion on this subject may open the door for a new-found jail ministry!

I cannot say enough—God loves the sinner but ***despises the sin.*** God has provided a way for sinners to rid themselves of their sin. Christ has made available the cloak of righteousness so people can live a new lifestyle of holiness, purity and power.

In a time when Christ is **not** being viewed by our culture as beautiful and glorious, we must not be intimidated from manifesting the beauty and glory of our Lord and Savior Jesus Christ. Under cultural pressure from a polytheistic (believing in many gods) society, Paul declared:

> I am not ashamed of the gospel, because it is the power of God for the salvation of ***everyone who believes....***
> —Romans 1:16 (NIV) EMPHASIS ADDED

Today many believers are actually ashamed of their relationship to Christ. Because Christ is not readily accepted in our communities, many believers are afraid to have Him accompany them to work or family gatherings. They keep their relationship with Jesus a secret. It's as though they are **under-cover** Christians.

> Whosoever therefore shall be **ashamed** of me and of my words in this adulterous and sinful generation; of him also shall the Son of man be **ashamed**, when he cometh in the glory of his Father with the holy angels.
> —Mark 8:38 EMPHASIS ADDED

Escaped of Israel

Isaiah 4:2 states that the Branch of the Lord is beautiful and glorious to those who "***are escaped of Israel.***" Israel, in Isaiah's time, had become a symbol of legalism and powerless religion. Throughout Isaiah, God consistently challenges Israel to seek Him with a pure heart.

They served God in a form and fashion that did not please Him. God began to despise their solemn meetings and their times of prayer and fasting (Isaiah 58). Numerous verses describe God's frustration with Israel. In chapter one He declares their garments were soiled with sin, yet they thought of themselves as pure and righteous. In chapter five God declares He had planted the Israelites in good soil, surrounded them with protection and had great expectations of receiving a harvest of good fruit. Yet, in disappointment and bewilderment He laments that they brought forth wild grapes. In Isaiah chapter fifty-five, God has simply had enough of their religious services, sacrifices and offerings.

Jesus confronted the same type of religious apostasy in His day. He actually quotes Isaiah to the Pharisees, rebuking them:

> ...you draw close to me with your lips (words of praise) but your hearts (passions, emotions and desires) are far from me.
>
> —Matthew 15:8

As bad as it was in Isaiah's day, there was still a small group of Jews sold out to God, and who longed to see Him high and lifted up. History, records that there is always a small pocket of believers committed to God during times of apostasy known as the remnant.

For instance, during the Babylonian rule under King Nebuchadnezzar, there was a remnant of young men hungry for God. Their names were Meshech, Shadrach, Abed-nego and Daniel. Though they found themselves in a land where God was not honored, where the religious institution had become unrighteous, where there was no difference between holy and unholy, nevertheless they were part of a small remnant of believers who would not yield to the pressures of culture. They were, in God's eyes, a remnant that remained hungry for the Lord.

There was also a remnant of believers in Nehemiah's day. Nehemiah wept when he saw the walls of Jerusalem knocked down. In his eyes the testimony of God had been trampled upon. His weeping started a grassroots movement, which sparked a remnant to rebuild the walls. In one of the most memorable accounts of passion and desire, Nehemiah and the remnant rebuilt the wall with a trowel in one hand and a sword in the other (Nehemiah 4:17).

The reference to the *escaped* in Isaiah's prophecy represents a *"present day remnant."* These believers escape the present powerless church and behold Jesus, the Branch, as beautiful and glorious. My heart leaps for joy that, in the midst of a crooked and perverse culture and a church that is in need of revival, there is a growing remnant of passionate believers who love Jesus above all else.

There is a growing remnant of passionate believers who love Jesus above all else.

Like Nehemiah and Daniel there is a growing number of pastors and churches longing to see God move. They hunger and thirst for revival. They consistently preach messages of righteousness and purity. At these churches marriages are being restored, strife-ridden homes are becoming unified, and people are being set free from bondages, addictions, fears, anxieties, depression, oppression and anger, just to name a few.

I have spoken to countless pastors around the country who are leading remnant churches and *restoring the hearts of the children to the hearts of the fathers and the hearts of the fathers to the hearts of the children* (Malachi 4:6). Young people who once contemplated leaving the church are catching a fire for His presence. These churches are being established as fountainheads of living water, attracting believers and sinners alike who are thirsty and hungry for Christ, the living water and the bread of heaven.

The "last day's" church will be filled with God's glory.

The Church of Great Power

The "last day's" church will be filled with God's glory. It will be more than just a forgiven church—it will be a holy church. It will have been purged with the consuming fire of God's convicting word. Holiness and purity will characterize the people.

> And it shall come to pass, that he that is left in Zion, and he that remaineth in Jerusalem, shall be called holy, even every one that is written among the living in Jerusalem ...
>
> —Isaiah 4:3

This is not referring to physical Jerusalem, but a new, heavenly Jerusalem, a spiritual city that is the "mother" of all believers.

> But Jerusalem which is above is free, which is the mother of us all.
>
> —Galatians 4:26

> But ye are come unto mount Sion, and unto the city of the living God, the ***"Heavenly Jerusalem,"*** and to an innumerable company of angels...
>
> —Hebrews 12:22 EMPHASIS ADDED

> ...the city of God, which is new Jerusalem, which cometh down out of heaven from God...
>
> —Revelation 3:12

A heavenly-minded remnant will be found in the New Jerusalem, made up of those whom the Lord will bring through His consuming fire. It will be the church that will inherit God's Glory.

This church recognizes the Branch (Jesus) as beautiful, glorious, and excellent. These believers will run toward Him. They will desire intimacy with Him. They will remove themselves from every other influence in order to be with ***this beautiful Branch, which is Jesus Christ the Lord and Savior!***

This message is for every pastor who has remained strong and not been swayed by public opinion, nor bent to the pressure to compromise the message of God in their hearts. You are the Nehemiahs and Daniels of our day. Sound the trumpet loud and clear! In the days to come God will raise you from obscurity. You will inherit the promises of Isaiah 58…

> Then shall thy light break forth as the morning, and thine health shall spring forth speedily: and thy righteousness shall go before thee; the glory of the LORD shall be thy reward. Then shalt thou call, and the LORD shall answer; thou shalt cry, and he shall say, Here I am. If thou take away from the midst of thee the yoke, the putting forth of the finger, and speaking vanity; And if thou draw out thy soul to the hungry, and satisfy the afflicted soul; then shall thy light rise in obscurity, and thy darkness be as the noonday: And the LORD shall guide thee continually, and satisfy thy soul in drought, and make fat thy bones: and thou shalt be like a watered garden, and like a spring of water, whose waters fail not.
>
> And they that shall be of thee shall build the old waste places: thou shalt raise up the foundations of many generations; and thou shalt be called, The repairer of the breach, The restorer of paths to dwell in. If thou turn away thy foot from the sabbath, from doing thy pleasure on my holy day; and call the sabbath a delight, the holy of the LORD, honourable; and shalt honour him, not doing thine own ways, nor finding thine own pleasure, nor speaking thine own words: Then shalt thou delight thyself in the LORD; and I will cause thee to ride upon the high places of the earth, and feed thee with the heritage of Jacob thy father: for the mouth of the LORD hath spoken it.
>
> —Isaiah 58:8-14

Continue to lift up Christ and behold the beauty of our Lord and Savior.

Because of the condition of the church, some will come and go in your congregations and you may experience hurt and perhaps be wounded. However, *do not be discouraged with the comings and goings of vagabond believers. Continue to lift up Christ and behold the beauty of our Lord and Savior.*

~5~

The Direction & Comfort of the Lord

How blessed is the man whose strength is in you, in whose heart are the highways to Zion! Passing through the valley of Baca they make it a spring; the early rain also covers it with blessings. They go from strength to strength, every one of them appear before God in Zion.

—Psalm 84: 5-7

And the LORD will create upon every dwelling place of mount Zion, and upon her assemblies, a cloud and smoke by day, and the shining of a flaming fire by night: for upon all the glory shall be a defense.

—Isaiah 4:5

The Direction & Comfort of the Lord

How blessed is the man whose strength is in you, in whose heart are the highways to Zion! Passing through the valley of Baca they make it a spring; the early rain also covers it with blessings. They go from strength to strength, every one of them appear before God in Zion.

—Psalm 84: 5-7

And the LORD will create upon every dwelling place of mount Zion, and upon her assemblies, a cloud and smoke by day, and the shining of a flaming fire by night: for upon all the glory shall be a defense.

—Isaiah 4:5

One of the attributes of God is faithfulness. When God makes a promise, He keeps it. He is not a man that He should lie (Numbers 23:19). When He speaks a word, it comes to pass. God's faithfulness was constant throughout King David's life. Whether as a young boy singing songs of praise, or fighting off the lion and the bear, God was with him. When he stood up to Israel's archenemy Goliath, God was at his side. When he fled to the caves of Adullam to escape Saul's murderous heart, and when as king fought countless battles, God never failed him. As David reflected upon his life, he knew, without doubt, that God was faithful.

> I have been young, and now am old; yet have I not seen the righteous forsaken, nor his seed begging bread.
> —Psalm 37:25

You can stake your life, and the lives of your family on His faithfulness.

Among all God's attributes, His faithfulness made the greatest impression on David's heart. God had even been faithful when David was not. Today, no matter how crooked this world gets, or how dark the culture may appear, ***God remains faithful.*** You can stake your life, and the lives of your family on His faithfulness. At times, when you do not see God's hand moving in your life, you can rest assured He is maneuvering behind the scenes and strategizing on your behalf. Whether Joseph was being sold into slavery or imprisoned in a dungeon, God was weaving a master plan to take him from the *pit to the palace.*

If you are a part of that remnant that feeds on His bread, is clothed in His righteousness and longs to see His appearing—you have ***nothing to fear.***

The Protection of God

In the perilous last days, God is going to provide, a cloud by day and a fire by night. This promise extends to every congregation and every individual who longs for Jesus.

The first appearance of this cloud occurs as the Israelites are escaping Egypt. Through the mighty hand of God, manifested by ten miracles, Israel was delivered from Egypt. However, the heart of Pharaoh was once again hardened toward Israel, causing him to send armies to destroy them. Israel, which had made its way to the Red Sea, was now quickly being cornered. With the Red Sea before them and the armies of Pharaoh behind them, the people of Israel became fearful, with no way of escape.

They were not warriors skilled in the art of battle. Actually, they were men, women, and children who were the descendants of eleven consecutive generations of slaves.[1] The Hebrews were accustomed to trowels, pitchforks and farming tools. Before God gives them a way of escape, He manifests His cloud and fire so that Israel can spend a night resting in His presence in the midst of her enemies.

> And it came between the camp of the Egyptians and the camp of Israel; and it was a cloud and darkness *to them (the Egyptians)*, but it gave light by night *to these (the Israelites)*: so that the one came not near the other all the night.
>
> —Exodus 14:20

All night long the Egyptians could not see one foot in front of another. The cloud cast them into utter darkness, disarray and confusion. At the same time, God turned on a night-light for Israel. God knows how to separate and protect His children from the children of this world!

God knows how to separate and protect His children from the children of this world!

This prophecy in Isaiah declares that the cloud and fire are made available today for those who are part of His remnant. As He did in those days, God continues to confuse the enemy's plans in our lives.

> Let mine adversaries be clothed with shame, and let them cover themselves with their own confusion, as with a mantle.
>
> —Psalm. 109:29

The Cloud and Fire Remained

God continued to keep the cloud by day and fire by night during Israel's treacherous journey through the wilderness. Throughout the Bible we see that the cloud provided many benefits—protection, guidance and a means through which God communicated with His people. For instance, the cloud covered them from the scorching wilderness sun. The wilderness Israel passed through was actually a desert with no water, rain, or vegetation. It was a barren climate not conducive to agriculture or the raising of livestock.

As the cloud moved, so the people of Israel packed up and moved their tents and belongings until the cloud hovered at a particular location, signifying the place God had prepared for His people. Nehemiah tells us the cloud and fire accompanied Israel for the next forty years in the wilderness. During that time the cloud changed the atmosphere so they could farm, produce crops, have plenty to drink and not merely survive, but thrive (Nehemiah 9:19-21).

In the New Testament this cloud appears at the baptism of Jesus. The voice of God spoke through the cloud, as Matthew's Gospel reports.

> … a bright ***cloud*** overshadowed them: and behold a voice out of the ***cloud***, which said, this is my beloved Son, in whom I am well pleased; hear ye him.
>
> —Matthew 17:5 EMPHASIS ADDED

Today God positions His cloud over His remnant churches—no

matter where they are located. Job 15:15 reveals that the heavens are unclean, and Paul noted that spiritual atmosphere of his day was resisting Kingdom expansion as well. In Ephesians 6:12 he wrote,

> ...we wrestle not against flesh and blood, but against principalities, against powers, against the rulers of the darkness of this world, against spiritual wickedness in high *places.*

God's cloud provides a barrier against the negative contemporary cultural atmosphere.

While lawlessness increases in our day, Isaiah declares that God's cloud will counteract the works of darkness and cause His people to flourish. From the suburbs to the cities, from developing nations to underground churches, God's cloud provides a barrier against the negative contemporary cultural atmosphere. Under this cloud of protection, we can experience communion with God and an open heaven. The cloud of God sets the atmosphere for the glory of the Lord to be revealed upon His congregations. In it is the supply of provision, protection, revival and renewal.

This Cloud Rains Revival

Beloved, God's cloud always comes with rain. In fact, a rainless cloud is a scriptural symbol of legalism and dead religion. Both Peter and Jude refer to the religious leaders of their days as clouds that bring no rain.

> ... clouds *they are* without water, driven by winds...
>
> —Jude 1:12

> These are wells without water, clouds that are carried with a tempest …
>
> —2 Peter 2:1

History shows that at the darkest of times, where the light of the church has dwindled, God pours out revival.

> In the light of the king's countenance *is* life; and His favor *is* as a ***cloud of the latter rain.***
>
> —Proverbs 16:15 EMPHASIS ADDED

From the sparks of the Reformation which led the church out of the dark ages, to the Columbian revival which broke the back of the drug cartel, to the Argentine Outpouring which destroyed legalism, He searches for a faithful remnant and there manifests His cloud and sends His rain of revival. I believe we are quickly approaching the day where we will see pockets of revival all across America.

> For the eyes of the LORD run to and fro throughout the whole earth, to shew himself strong in the behalf of *them* whose heart *is* perfect toward him…
>
> —2 Chronicles 16:9

Now is the time to pray and cultivate a hunger to see God move in our lives, churches and communities.

The Fire of God

Isaiah's prophecy tells us that a "flaming fire" will accompany the cloud.

As in times past, God will make available a fire of purification. At first glance this may not seem appealing, yet a closer look will uncover how vital and necessary it is.

More troubling than backslidden individuals is the backslidden condition of the church.

Over the last twenty years of ministry I have witnessed believers backslide whom I thought would never fall away from God. There's nothing surprising about believers backsliding. Even among Jesus' original twelve apostles, Judas betrayed Jesus, Peter denied Him and James and John had misplaced priorities. But what is more troubling than backslidden individuals is the backslidden condition of the church. The moral standard of the church in the 21st century is at an alarming all-time low.

This backslidden condition has diminished the quality of the believer. It's as though the church has lowered the bar that Christ set Himself. Reducing the standard has become an accepted cultural antidote to solving difficult problems. In the educational system, for example, if students cannot master the content of a grade level the standard is lowered. The same is true for firefighters, police officers, and other public servants. Inferior standards weaken every endeavor where they are accepted. As a direct consequence of lowering the standards of our educational system, we are not preparing the next generation of workers and leaders for doing business internationally. Yet, in countries like Japan, where education is a value woven into society, there is a quest for *raising the bar.*

Because of this diluted gospel many in the church today are spiritually and morally anemic and malnourished.

Unfortunately, the church's response has been the same— lowering the bar to accommodate a lower level of commitment. The Bible refers to this as a lukewarm commitment or a spirit of mediocrity. Because of this diluted gospel many in the church today are spiritually and morally anemic and malnourished. Christianity has been so watered down that there is in some facets of the church no distinct difference between the church and secular society. Nothing shocks us—even within the church.

C.S. Lewis put it this way:

> We have lost the invaluable faculty of being shocked—a faculty which has hitherto almost distinguished the Man or Woman from the beast or child.[2]

Churches are not leading people into a deeper experience of transformation in Christ.

A Place of Transformation

Churches are not leading people into a deeper experience of transformation in Christ. All too often, church leaders are happy just to see people come to church and give tithes and offerings. Many believers are in church on Sunday and at the casinos or nightclubs throughout the week. Many in the church have become "carnival cruisers" looking for social life and personal gratification, but not holiness.

Church used to be the place where people were delivered, set free, filled with the Holy Ghost and empowered to live the Christian life. We can even see this apostasy in the Christian literature of our day. Self-help and motivation has taken the place of holiness and purity in many popular Christian books. The most respected and revered Christian authors prior to 1970 stressed holiness, righteousness and a distinct call to be separate and sanctified.

The condition of spirituality in our society is dictating the quality of commitment in the lives of many believers. Our nation is fast becoming a dry and parched land—a place where true spiritual food is not sought. Consequently, this has resulted in weak, apathetic and immature believers. Billy Graham, commenting on the loss of our moral compass, had this to say:

> *We've lost sight of the fact that some things are always right and some things are always wrong. We've lost our reference point. We don't have any moral philosophy to under gird our way of life in this country, and our way of life is in serious jeopardy and serious danger unless something happens. And that something must be a spiritual revival.*[3]

The Tipping Point

The tipping point of this backslidden condition occurred during the Clinton administration, when a President of the United States used the Oval Office for sexual encounters with an intern. Not only did President Clinton commit blatant sin, he then adamantly denied it. Yet polls showed the majority of Americans did not think his private life had anything to do with his ability to lead. This separation of a leader's private life from his public life is hypocrisy. We justify duality as though it were natural. The now famous statement—*"I did not have sex with that woman*— made on worldwide television stands as a testament to our cultural apostasy. The ensuing argument over whether oral sex was the equivalent of adultery or fornication should have been an insult to the moral intelligence of any thinking individual. Could this have been the forerunner of the "friends with benefits" philosophy plaguing our young people and the sexual immorality and promiscuity of our culture? I wonder if the President's disregard for the covenant of marriage allowed many to justify their own affairs.

On May 24, 1800, William Paterson stated:

> *Religion and morality...are necessary to good government, good order, and good laws...*

King Solomon said:

> ...when the righteous are in authority, the people rejoice: but when the ***wicked*** beareth rule, the people mourn
>
> —Proverbs 29:2 EMPHASIS ADDED

The church is in need of the purging fire of God.

John Maxwell, the noted management expert, rightly observes, "Everything rises and falls on leadership." If that is true, then having the leader of our country engage in sexual misconduct could very well have accelerated the release of a spirit of compromise, apathy and hypocrisy into our nation. As churches begin to mirror the culture and become more apt to break God's laws and covenants, when the people of God become indifferent and apathetic towards the word of God, when we do not hearken or comply with God's standards, when we are contemptuous and rejecting of God's statutes and despise His moral laws, then the church is in need of the purging fire of God.

Victory Over Sin

> *Revival is a sovereign act of God upon the church whereby he intervenes to lift the situation completely out of human hands and works in extraordinary power.*[4] *(Geoffrey R. King)*

Isaiah says God will make His reviving fire available to assemblies and believers who eat His bread, wear His apparel and love His appearing. One of the characteristics of true revival is victory over sin. Sin will no longer hold these congregations captive and bound, for the fire of God will purge their sin, empty works, and mediocrity.

> *The greatest miracle that God can do today is to take an unholy man out of an unholy world, and make that man holy and put him back into that unholy world and keep him holy in it.*[5] *(Leonard Ravenhill, 1908–1996)*

This fire will boil the complacency out of the church and ignite a passion for His presence. This is the signature of Jesus' ministry.

> I indeed (John the Baptist) baptize you with water unto repentance: but he that cometh after me is mightier than I, whose shoes I am not worthy to bear: he shall baptize you with the Holy Ghost, and ***with fire***...
>
> —Matthew 3:11 EMPHASIS ADDED

To eliminate the "Baptism of Fire" from the gospel message is to negate the power of purification. This leaves the believer attending church, yet enslaved to sin. For he may have the *"will"* to do good but lack the firepower to bring it about. Christian author Frank Damazio states that:

> "When God comes down, He burns into our spirits a new love and excitement for Him. A burning zeal and a new enthusiasm surfaces in us when God comes down.[6]"

If you have never experienced the Baptism of Fire, if you are struggling to maintain your salvation, rarely ever experiencing breakthrough, then pray for God to open the heavens above your head and send His consuming fire to liberate, revive and ignite a spiritual passion within you.

~6~

The Butterfly Effect

Science tells us that even the most insignificant actions can cause extreme results.

The "butterfly effect" states that the tiny air disturbance from the flapping of a butterfly's wings can ultimately lead to a dramatic storm.

And there shall be a tabernacle for a shadow in the daytime
from the heat, and for a place of refuge,
and for a covert from storm and from rain.

—Isaiah 4:6

The Butterfly Effect

Science tells us that even the most insignificant actions can cause extreme results.

The "butterfly effect" states that the tiny air disturbance from the flapping of a butterfly's wings can ultimately lead to a dramatic storm.

And there shall be a tabernacle for a shadow in the daytime from the heat, and for a place of refuge, and for a covert from storm and from rain.

—Isaiah 4:6

This verse gives insight into our contemporary climate. The reference to storms implies there will be a great need for God's protection. Storms in scripture come in both the natural and spiritual realm, and even a skeptic can see something is happening in the earth's atmosphere.

Many scientists believe a contributing factor to the increase of natural disasters is the "Greenhouse Effect", also known as global warming.[1] They suggest global warming is causing atmospheric changes and unpredictable weather patterns. Whatever the case, we live in a time where we regularly see devastating hurricanes, killer tornadoes, and deadly flooding. However, we must be very careful not to attribute all these events to God's judgment on the earth.

We see in scripture the judgment of God on nations such as Sodom and Gomorrah, Nineveh and many others. God always reserves the right to judge a nation. Yet, I would be very hesitant to attribute any catastrophe or calamity to the hand of God. The scriptures portray God as quick to forgive, restore and revive, yet longsuffering, patient and forbearing in judgment. Moses and David, two of the men closest to God, proclaimed the fervent lovingkindess and patience of the Lord.

> And the Lord passed by before him, and proclaimed, the Lord, the Lord God, merciful and gracious, longsuffering, and abundant in goodness and truth, Keeping mercy for thousands, forgiving iniquity and transgression and sin…
>
> —Exodus 34:6,7

> But thou, O Lord, *art* a God full of compassion, and gracious, longsuffering, and plenteous in mercy and truth.
>
> —Psalm 86:15

History records that the judgment or discipline of God, is used as a last resort. In my opinion, ninety-nine percent of people's problems are not the result of God's judgment; rather they are the result of people making bad decisions. Man still has not learned the principle of cause and effect—every action sets in motion a reaction! Despite popular opinion that God puts us into jams and difficulties, the fact is He spends more time getting us out of them.

Despite popular opinion that God puts us into jams and difficulties, the fact is He spends more time getting us out of them.

Cataclysmic Events

Science seems to be telling us that humans, not God, are causing cataclysmic events. Could it be that man's relentless consumption of the earth's resources is causing irreversible problems in our world? Perhaps the near extinction of tropical rainforests, the depletion of earth's minerals, the consumption of fossil fuels, and tampering with the balance of nature is sending shock waves through the Earth.

For instance, in the animal kingdom there is an increase in attacks on humans as species are driven out of their habitats by urban sprawl. When people move their homes into areas once reserved for animals, the creatures are forced to become aggressive to survive. Is that the fault of the animals or of the people taking away their natural habitat? God is not causing the animals to attack. The actions of people are to blame.

Mankind is the only creature that does not respect the balance of nature. Look at our polluted rivers and lakes, once pristine and inviting, now filled with toxins from years of dumping chemical waste—without regard for the impact on aquatic life.

If the earth is created by God and man consistently tampers, depletes and shows no regard for the planet—what would be the earth's natural response? It would probably call for its creator to come and set the balance straight again. Could it be that humanity has so afflicted the earth that it longs for Christ's return? This is exactly what the Bible states in Romans 8:22, which says, "For we know that the whole creation groaneth and travaileth in pain together until now."

Is it possible that all creation is crying out for the creator?

Could this groaning be everything from earthquakes to storms to natural tragedies? Is it possible that all creation is crying out for the creator? At the crucifixion of Jesus, not only were Mary, the mother of Jesus, and Mary Magdalene crying, but it seems that all of creation was weeping as well. The Bible records:

> Now from the sixth hour there was ***darkness*** over all the land unto the ninth hour.
>
> —Matthew 27:45 EMPHASIS ADDED

> And, behold, the veil of the temple was rent in twain from the top to the bottom; and the ***earth did quake***, and the ***rocks rent***; and the graves were opened; and many bodies of the saints which slept arose…
>
> —Matthew 27:51-53 EMPHASIS ADDED

One of the clearest indications that this report is unbiased comes from a non-believing Roman soldier who witnessed the earth's response to the death of Christ.

> Now when the centurion, and they that were with him, watching Jesus, ***saw the earthquake***, and those things that were done, they feared greatly, saying, truly this was the Son of God.
>
> —Matthew 27:54 EMPHASIS ADDED

Nature always responded to Jesus. Satan attempted to use the storms to kill Jesus, but Jesus calmed the storms. The water yielded to His presence and became solid under His feet so He could walk on it. Jesus predicted the increase of wars, famines, pestilence, and earthquakes as a sign of His return (Matthew 24:4-14).

Author Grant R. Jeffrey states:

> Since A.D. 1900, the growth in major earthquakes has been

> relentless. From 1900 to 1949, it averaged three major quakes per decade. From 1949, the increase became awesome with 9 killer quakes in the 1950's; 13 in the 60's; 56 in the 1970's and an amazing 74 major quakes in the 1980's. Finally, in the 1990's, the number topped 100. (Source: U.S. Geological Survey Earthquake Report, Boulder, Colorado). [2]

Beloved, the Earth is so abused; it travails, awaiting the coming of our Lord and Savior Jesus Christ.

The Butterfly Effect

Anything that happens in one part of nature has the potential to affect the whole. Our actions never take place in a void, but always generate ripple effects. Science tells us that even the most insignificant things in life can result in major impacts. The "*butterfly effect*" states that the tiny air disturbance from the flapping of a butterfly's wings can ultimately lead to a dramatic storm. Apply the "*butterfly effect*" to the removal of the acknowledgement of God from a society and the results are devastating. The eruption of spiritual storms in our culture is nothing more than the reaction to the decision to remove God's influence from every aspect of our way of life.

Our actions never take place in a void, but always generate ripple effects.

One way to understand this is to think what would happen if a city's police department were removed. Though there's not a police officer on every corner, or a police station in every neighborhood, the presence of a police department in a city keeps criminal activity at bay. It is a deterrent to many would-be criminals. So, while God may not have been in every home, His manifest presence in a community would still be a deterrent to sin and lawlessness.

Our nation witnessed this very situation in the aftermath of Hurricane Katrina. The storm paralyzed the New Orleans police department, and every sinful act imaginable was committed. I am not talking about people taking bread to feed their families but about rape, unbridled violence and murder.

The consequences of removing God from the school system are undeniable.

There are major consequences when a society takes God out of the picture. When a school system serves God with a notice to vacate, we should not be surprised that what takes His place is a plague on our children.

The consequences of removing God from the school system are undeniable. In 1962 and 1963, two decisions were made that forever changed the moral climate of the public schools in our country. Respected author and historian David Barton put it this way:

> In decisions rendered on June 25, 1962, in *Engel v Vitale*, and on June 17, 1963, in *Murray v Curlett and Abington v Schempp*, the ***Supreme Court forbade*** the inclusion of religious activities in major activities of daily student life by striking down ***school prayer*** and ***Bible reading***. Never before in the history of our nation had any branch of our government taken such a stand. Through those decisions, thirty-nine million students and over two million teachers were barred from participating in what had been available to students since our nation's founding. Even today, millions of Americans personally recall when prayer, Bible reading, and religious principles were as much a part of their public school activities as was the study of math or the pursuit of athletics. Activities once considered an integral part of education are now totally censured.[3]

The following factual list gives you a clear picture of the "butterfly effect" after those horrendous decisions were made.

- Birth rates for unwed girls 15-19 years of age tripled
- Pregnancies among unwed girls under 15 years of age quadrupled
- Pregnancies among unwed girls 15-19 years of age reached seven times the level recorded prior to the removal of prayer from schools
- Sexually transmitted disease increased 300%

Dramatic changes in student morality were not the only changes in student life following those Supreme Court decisions. Before the ban on religious teachings, the top public school problems were listed as: talking, chewing gum, making noise, running in the halls, getting out of turn in line, wearing improper clothing and not putting paper in wastebaskets.

The courts have judged the public schools and our children are paying the price.

Polls now list the top offenses as: rape, robbery, assault, burglary, arson, bombings, murder, suicide, absenteeism, vandalism, extortion, drug abuse, alcohol abuse, gang warfare, pregnancies, abortions, and venereal disease. [4]

So significant were the changes in student behavior following the Court decisions, that by 1965 the U.S. Department of Justice began to track youth violence as ***a separate category***—something not previously done.

So, then, is God judging the public schools? *No*! The courts have judged the public schools and our children are paying the price.

Students today are being exposed to a cesspool of sin.

Higher Education?

Consider higher education. Instead of getting a "higher" education many students today are being exposed to a cesspool of sin. I am not limiting this to the immoral activities of Spring Break. I am talking about the everyday experience of many college students in this nation. You do not have to be a Christian to be concerned about what your children are being taught on college campuses across America. Any moral person who looks closely at what is going on should be disgusted by what is taking place under the guise of higher education. College professors are increasingly using their positions to indoctrinate rather than educate.

Twenty years ago, this was not a concern considering there was an equal amount of liberal and conservative professors. Statistics today indicate that the numbers are dangerously skewed toward liberal bias in the ranks of college professors. As much as eighty percent of college professors today are considered to be liberal and that is reflected in the types of courses being offered.

Students are offered more and more bizarre and biased courses that reflect the narrow ideology of liberal professors. Courses in which the faculty ***imposes*** its views on race, sex, economics, history and politics are not only proliferating, but are increasingly becoming required to receive degrees.

> Yale University offers: Introduction to Lesbian and Gay Studies: "A study of works that have as their theme gay and lesbian experience and identity in the 20th-century United States."
>
> The University of Michigan offers How to be Gay: Male Homosexuality and Initiation: "Just because you

> happen to be a gay man doesn't mean that you don't have to learn how to become one." As if the pervading pro-homosexual atmosphere on college campuses isn't enough of an education.
>
> Bucknell University offers Witchcraft and Politics: Explores witchcraft, spirit possession, and cults of the dead as idioms of power and as vehicles for protest, resistance, and violent social change.

While instruction about the failed history of Marxism and its negative effects on nations is worthwhile instruction in a college history class, the promotion of disastrous political ideology should never occur. Not so, according to many prominent colleges around the nation. Courses with a distinctly pro-Marxist agenda are currently offered at universities such as Brown, Cornell, Princeton, Duke and on and on the list goes. Amherst College even offers Taking Marx Seriously, while the University of California at Santa Barbara offers Black Marxism.

Tomorrow's world is being shaped, to a very large extent, by today's teachers.

> At UC-Berkley, they have all sorts of naughty fun in class. One course…concerning male sexuality made national headlines. All the students in the co-ed class publicly discussed their sexual fantasies. Porn stars guest lectured… during another class assignment, students went to a gay strip club…At Mount Holyoke College in Massachusetts, Prof. Susan Scotto teaches students how to strip in her stripping course. The mother of two, strips at local bars in her spare time. For the final assignment of Prof. Hope Weissman's 1999-2000 pornography and politics course at Wesleyan University, students were told to "create your own work of pornography." Students presented their assignments to the class via self-made video or, if they so wished, live in front of the class![5]

The Ten Suggestions

You might wonder how such things could ever happen in American colleges. Is there no conviction? Is there no understanding of moral excellence? No! It was removed when God was asked to leave and take prayer and the Ten Commandments with Him. In place of absolute law and His moral standard is the liberal philosophy of "moral relativism."

You might wonder how such things could ever happen in American colleges.

Moral relativism is the belief that defining right and wrong is an individual and rational choice. Denying the presence of absolute law, this ideology teaches that every decision is a matter of personal feeling. Moral relativism means that adultery, for example, is not objectively wrong. While I may believe that adultery is wrong and that it destroys marriages, you are entitled to believe it is right and strengthens a marriage. The same reasoning applies for murder, stealing, pedophilia and every other facet of human life. With this ideology, there is no absolute definition of right and wrong—only what you *perceive* to be right and wrong. This distorted principle has made great inroads into our universities. Created by secularists, moral relativism is a by-product of the evolutionist theory, which itself permeates university culture, especially the sciences. By denying the existence of God, the theory of evolution sowed the seeds of moral relativism. If there is no God, secularists reason, then there is no absolute law. Using moral relativism as their weapon, liberal secularists can destroy any absolute law they desire. Even the laws that govern society can be destroyed. Most people recognize that American law, ideology and morals are essentially governed by Judeo-Christian belief in the Ten Commandments. Since there is no

God, according to secularists, then all we have are ten suggestions. There is no law. With no absolute laws, defining right and wrong is a strictly personal matter.

Removing God, Removes Protection

When you eliminate God's presence in every aspect of community, you instantly allow lawlessness to increase. In effect, by our own hand, we are causing judgment to fall. God is blamed for every disaster that comes about but in reality, we are to blame because we have put God out of our midst. When God is removed so is His protecting presence. "In the absence of light darkness will ***always*** prevail!"

In effect, by our own hand, we are causing judgment to fall.

The responsibility falls on us for rejecting God and not making Him welcome anymore. Storms that once missed us now hit us because the shelter of His presence is not there to protect us. When a nation has lost its purpose—all things ***no longer*** work out for good. God does not necessarily cause the storms (tragedies, difficulties, terror, etc.) to hit us. Yet, in the absence of His presence things that might have missed us hit us head on.

Jesus stands on the banks of our country weeping over this back-slidden nation. He longs to see her return to her roots,

"One Nation Under God, Indivisible,
With Liberty and Justice For All."

~7~

The Glory of the Lord

For I, saith the LORD, will be unto her a wall of fire round about, and will be the ***glory*** *in the midst of her.*

—Zechariah 2:5

...for upon all ***the glory shall be a defense.*** *And there shall be a tabernacle for a shadow in the daytime from the heat, and for a* ***place of refuge.***

—Isaiah 4:5.6 EMPHASIS ADDED

The Glory of the Lord

For I, saith the LORD, will be unto her a wall of fire round about, and will be the ***glory*** *in the midst of her.*

—Zechariah 2:5

...for upon all ***the glory shall be a defense.*** *And there shall be a tabernacle for a shadow in the daytime from the heat, and for a* ***place of refuge.***

—Isaiah 4:5.6 EMPHASIS ADDED

The person trusting in God has a *"defense"* and a *"refuge,"* says Isaiah. If that is the case, why do so many believers act as though they were defenseless? Could it be that they do not *fully* understand the glorious presence of God? Even more devastating is the growing *disregard* for the presence of God. Believers have become satisfied with just one aspect of His presence. The manifest presence of God has all but evaporated from most church services, functions and gatherings, replaced with famous preachers, and paid musicians.

Regrettably, the church in our day has become big business. Some churches are larger in attendance than the population of small towns. Do not get me wrong; I am not opposed to mega churches. However,

Regrettably, the church in our day has become big business.

shouldn't larger churches mean the mobilization of considerable Christian resources to ***transform*** communities, cities and infuse Kingdom values in our culture?

Instead, churches spend more money on keeping people saved than on saving new people. This has created an alternative culture for Christians where they are not required to be clothed in His righteousness, nor partake of the bread of life. No longer will a believer have to miss the fun and games, because they are readily available in church. Even the message of the 21st century church has shifted dramatically. It is almost exclusively focused on helping people cope. Some of the most notable preachers have adopted the philosophies, teachings and concepts of the self-help world.

Today, many ministries model themselves after local "Wal-mart" stores becoming what I call "Church-marts." They provide everything for which Christian hoppers, shoppers and "seeker" consumers can think of.

Many are loosing sight of the ***purpose*** of church and the ***passion*** of believers. It is the ***"Presence of God"*** that should be the heart's desire of every Christian. Jesus Christ high and lifted up should be the passion of every church.

It is the "Presence of God" that should be the heart's desire of every Christian.

The church is functioning properly when it is on fire for the Lord, and when the presence of Christ is the focus of its corporate life. When His manifest presence evaporates from the local church, or any Christian gathering, the assembly becomes dry, mechanical and self-absorbed.

1st Century Phenomena

Why is it that churches the sizes of cities are impotent to reproduce their values and beliefs in their communities? Could it be that these churches while enormous in size, still lack an important ingredient that was present in the New Testament church?

Acts records how the apostles accomplished their ministries with limited resources. They traveled on horseback, camels and chariots. They waited months to arrange travel upon ships, and spent weeks at sea on dangerous waters. It took these types of journeys to spread the gospel from one country, province, and city to another. They preached and planted churches with no completed Bible text. Without sound systems, stages, choirs or worship leaders, they turned their world upside down (Acts 17:6). The apostles had no marketing strategies, door hangers, or printed materials. When entering a new area that had not heard the Gospel of Jesus Christ it took only two disciples—not hundreds—to produce fruit and change a whole region. With no 21st century tools or studies of demographics, the Scriptures and history testify to the power that accompanied these men.

> "...These that have turned the world upside down are come hither also..."
>
> —Acts 17:6

How could as little as two disciples with no "state-of-the-art" resources have such power to change their world? Because they had something currently missing from many mainstream Christian churches—the ***"Manifest Presence of God."*** The reason it is missing from the church today is because believers have not been educated about His presence, nor do they realize it is readily available to them.

The Scriptures describe three aspects of the presence of God. They are the "omnipresence," the "indwelling" presence and the "manifest" presence.

The Omnipresence of the Lord

The first aspect of God's presence is referred to as the omnipresence. The omnipresence of God simply means that God is everywhere all the time. At first glance, this may be confusing for most readers. It would be important to appreciate that we know in part and that His wisdom is too awesome for us to fully comprehend. This is why Scripture tells us to "*lean not on our own understanding*"(Proverbs 3:5). In addition, "*His wisdom is too wonderful for me*" (Psalm. 139:6).

Let us consider the omnipresence of the Lord. Paul writing to the Colossians stated:

> For by Him were all things created, that are in heaven, and that are in earth, visible and invisible, whether they be thrones, or dominions, or principalities, or powers: all things were created by Him, and for him:
>
> —Colossians 1:16

This verse declares that all things are created by God. Within this passage is the key to unlocking the understanding of His omnipresence. The Scripture refers to God as the creator. If He is the creator, then what He creates will always contain His reflection.

The Image and Reflection of God

This is not uncommon even in our world. Every painting is a reflection of the artist. Every song is a reflection of the songwriter. And every building is a reflection of its builder and architect. This connection is so strong between creators and their creations, that even unsigned works, reveal their creator's signature. The works of people such as Mozart, Beethoven, Picasso, Van Gogh, Hemingway, Faulkner, and Frank Lloyd Wright declare the unmistakable attributes of their originators. In the field of forensic authenticity it is stated that an item can be associated with a particular creator because of the "inclusionary attributes" which amount to a reflection or authentic signature. These attributes are clearly discernable. In the same way, everything that God has created reveals His image. This is exactly what Paul says in the book of Romans stating:

> For ***the invisible things of Him from the creation of the world are clearly seen***, being understood by the things that are made, even his eternal power and Godhead; so that they are without excuse:
>
> —Romans 1:20 EMPHASIS ADDED

Like the brush of a painter and the clay of a sculptor, so God used all of creation as a canvas to paint a picture of His image. From the Grand Canyon to Niagara Falls, and from the mountains of Everest to Kilimanjaro, all of creation clearly contains the attributes of its creator. This leaves man without excuse.

Let me relate a personal experience that demonstrates how the omnipresence of God can be found in His creation.

> At a routine eye exam with my optometrist, our conversation took a unique turn. While in the chair, he asked me what I do for a living. I responded, "I'm a minister." He then proceeded to tell me that he found God in optometry. "How's that", I asked? He replied, "Well in the study of the way the eyes process color, you find that nature is completely suited to the way we see." He went on to ask, "Do you know why the sky is blue? "No", I said. He then told me, "It's the easiest color on the eyes." "Do you know why the grass is arrayed in green?" Once again I said, "No." He said, "because out of your peripheral vision green is the most distinguishable color." And he explained a series of things that he believed God did in the landscape of creation so our eyes can behold the image of His beauty. He concluded by saying, "*and that's how I found God in optometry.*"

The Psalmist agrees with my optometrist.

> The heavens declare the glory of God; the skies proclaim the work of His hands.
>
> —Psalm. 19:1 NIV

The fact is, God is reflected in all of his creation. Jeremiah asks the question:

> Can any hide himself in secret places that I shall not see him? Saith the LORD. Do not I fill heaven and earth saith the LORD?
>
> —Jeremiah 23:24

The Psalmist concludes that there is no place he can go to escape the presence of the Lord. He says:

> "Whither shall I flee from thy presence? If I ascend up into heaven, thou *art* there: if I make my bed in hell, behold, thou *art there. If* I take the wings of the morning, *and* dwell in the uttermost parts of the sea; even there shall thy hand lead me, and thy right hand shall hold me..."
>
> —Psalm 139: 5–11

This verse can only be understood through the three aspects of God's presence. The Psalmist is actually stating that if he were to end up in hell, even there he would find the presence of God. Now, I assure you that God is **NOT** in hell. The Bible states that God is sitting on His throne surrounded by twenty-four elders who continually sing praises to His name. So then what is the Psalmist referring to when he states that even in hell he would find God's presence? He is referring to the *omnipresence* of the Lord. This now makes sense when you consider that, since hell was created by God, it too reflects the image of God.

And those who end up there will always be reminded, by His reflection, that they have rejected Him.

This can be extended even further looking at the creation of man. When God created man He said, "*let us create him in our image and likeness*" (Genesis 1:26). This explains why we are the object of Satan's hatred. When he looks at man he sees the reflection of God and it infuriates him.

Nature, in all of its wonder, is also a reflection of God. His image is stamped throughout. Unfortunately, in many man-made religions they worship the object apart from God. This is fueled by the enemy of our soul. Throughout history we see the worship of trees, sun, moon, sky and even animals. Because these are a reflection of God, the enemy has been able to deceive people into worshiping the object rather than the creator. For the believer, the good news is that no matter where you look you can always find God. For it was in the woods of Albany that Charles Finney communed with God, felt His presence, fueled his prayer life and released his anxieties and cares. Even our Lord and Savior consistently drew apart from the chaotic cares of ministry and life to nature's tranquil settings. It is here He prayed and communed with His Father. In the Bible we find Jesus praying in mountains, gardens, seashores, and forests.

I encourage you on a starry night to look up and behold His omnipresence. Or take a stroll through the woods on a beautiful day and worship as the birds sing their praises to God.

The Indwelling Presence of God

This is the second aspect of the presence of God. It is given to every believer who has accepted Jesus Christ as Lord and Savior. At the moment a sinner is converted to Christ the Holy Spirit becomes resident in his or her life. The book of Ephesians states:

> "In whom ye also trusted, after that ye heard the word of truth, the gospel of your salvation: in whom also after that ye believed, *ye were sealed with that Holy Spirit of promise...*"
>
> —Ephesians 1:13 EMPHASIS ADDED

Consistently yielding to the Holy Spirit is vital to the "activating" of the indwelling presence of God.

As we yield to the Holy Spirit, the indwelling presence of God begins to permeate those areas that are submitted. It is the indwelling presence of God that produces His character and His nature in our lives. When properly yielded to it will produce tremendous fruit. The presence of God can be cultivated through prayer, worship, fasting, and many other disciplines associated with the Christian life. In addition, the disciplines of hungering after His word and being clothed in His righteousness produce a manifold increase of His presence. Consistently yielding to the Holy Spirit is vital to the "activating" of the indwelling presence of God.

We can develop the indwelling presence of God or hinder its development by resisting His promptings. The believer is warned not to "grieve" the Holy Spirit.

> "And grieve not the holy Spirit of God, whereby ye are sealed unto the day of redemption."
>
> —Ephesians 4:30

David prayed that God would not take His Holy Spirit from him.

> "Cast me not away from thy presence, and take not thy Holy Spirit from me..."
>
> —Psalm 51:11

The indwelling presence of the Lord is sometimes taken for granted. We know that God promises to "abide in us" (John 15). However, too often we stop there. As in all things the principle of sowing and reaping applies. The more we sow the more we reap. We are called to develop and deepen our understanding and relationship to the indwelling presence of God.

The Manifest Presence of God

The third aspect of God's presence is called the *"manifest"* presence of God. This is when God reveals Himself, usually by sovereign ways and means. This presence can be felt, even when one is not seeking God, or practicing spiritual disciplines such as prayer and repentance.

History records that at times, a strange sense of God pervaded buildings, communities, or districts. Many people have written articles or testified to feeling this awesome, sovereign presence of God in different locations.

In his book, *Seasons of Revival*, Frank Damazio tells the following story:

> "In 1858, during the American revivals, as ships drew near the American ports, they seemed to come under the influence of God's Spirit. Ship after ship arrived in America with the same accounts of sudden conviction and conversion. This was the sovereign presence of God being manifested in a situation or a circumstance where God Himself has initiated His presence upon people."[1]

Unfortunately, in our day the manifest presence of God is not the passion of believers and congregations across America. This is due to a lack of understanding about the presence of God.

I find there are very few believers and congregations praying for God to manifest His presence. It's as though many believers have been made aware of the availability of the indwelling presence of the Lord, but are unaware or uninterested in the other modes of His presence. It is as though we have eliminated two thirds of the glorious presence of the Lord.

Most believers do not pray for the manifest presence of God because they only understand the indwelling presence. They say, "We do not need to pray for His *manifest* presence, His presence is already manifested in us." They are referring, however, to the "indwelling" presence and not the "manifest" presence.

I cannot stress enough what a mistake that is! In times past, while the believer knew that God dwelt in him, there was a tremendous passion for God to dwell "around" him as well.

Moses spent forty days and forty nights on Mount Sinai in the manifest presence God. Afterward he returned to the camps of Israel, not realizing that his face now glowed with the presence of God. The manifest presence was so intense that Aaron and the Israelites became afraid to draw close to Moses. They eventually requested that Moses wear a veil (Exodus 34:28-33).

Believers should earnestly pray for the manifest presence of God to be upon their lives and households.

An over emphasis on one aspect of His presence is exactly what the enemy of our soul desires. Satan will happily allow you to serve God as long as you do not affect or influence his kingdom. He understands that light displaces darkness. The fact is, under his control evil pervades many buildings, streets, cities, and sometimes nations. It may seem incomprehensible, but many years ago, the leaders of the nation of Haiti actually dedicated their island to satan. From then on witchcraft, voodoo, and the occult have dominated the island and produced disastrous results. I have driven down city blocks and streets where I have distinctly felt the presence of evil. Yet, one street over this evil presence was lifted.

This is why satan would rather have believers consumed and focused on the indwelling presence rather than the manifest presence. He has seen what can happen when a handful of believers pray for God to manifest His presence. Cities are impacted, communities are changed, households are saved and the power of God is felt in a region.

Am I The Church?

This over emphasis on the indwelling presence has created many false conceptions. Some professed Christians say, "*we don't go to church,* because *we are the church.*" However, nowhere in the Bible is a believer referred to or addressed as a church. In Scripture, the church refers to the totality of believers. Other common names for the church are congregation, sheepfold, family of God and the body of Christ. Jesus did not write to ***seven believers*** in the book of Revelation, but to ***seven churches*** that represented the whole body.

This may sound new to contemporary doctrine, but it was completely understood by the Apostles and New Testament church. In fact, the idea of the church as the community of His manifest presence had been held throughout history until the mid-1970s when the "lay renewal" movement started. While some aspects of this movement were good, like teaching that God has called and gifted every believer for service, others were not. One particular teaching took the premise that the individual believer becomes solely the habitation of God, and not the church. This was expanded to the belief that every believer *is* the church. This position was widely popularized due to the growing independent spirit and self-centeredness within the church. Scriptures given to support this position stated that God no longer dwelt in buildings made with hands (Acts 7:48). Those Scripture references apply to the indwelling presence and not the manifest presence of God.

The Kingdom Structure

This error of referencing the believer as the church can be better understood by examining the structure of a company. If I were an employee of a company such as GE, I would receive many benefits—salary, benefit package, retirement program to name a few.

However, under no circumstances could I say that "I am" GE. While I work for the company, I am NOT the company. In fact, if I were to be removed from my position I would simultaneously lose all the residual benefits of being an employee of that company. The company always takes precedence over its employees. It is always the company that sets the standards, values, vision, mission, and purpose. It is the employee's responsibility to adhere to those core beliefs. Likewise, in the kingdom, the church takes precedence over the individual believer.

Jesus confirms this position in His instruction for conflict between believers,

> Moreover if thy brother shall trespass against thee, go and tell him his fault between thee and him alone: if he shall hear thee, thou hast gained thy brother. But if he will not hear *thee, then* take with thee one or two more, that in the mouth of two or three witnesses every

> word may be established. And if he shall neglect to hear them, ***tell it unto the church***: but if he neglect to hear the church, let him be unto thee as an heathen man and a publican.
>
> —Matthew 18:15-17 EMPHASIS ADDED

Jesus views the believer and the church as two separate entities. He declares that the church is *the* God appointed authority, which the believer must submit too.

I am not diminishing the position of the believer. Instead, I am emphasizing the importance of the believer being in proper alignment to the church. God designed His body to be interdependent not independent.

Corporate Benefits

His presence on a congregation is much different from His presence in a believer.

We are missing tremendous benefits by adhering to a false doctrine that alienates us from a corporate anointing. His presence on a congregation is much different from His presence in a believer.

It is essential to have an individual anointing, but there is a vast difference between an individual anointing and a corporate anointing. The Bible declares, "Again I say unto you, that if ***two of you*** shall agree on earth as touching any thing that they shall ask, it shall be done for them of my Father which is in heaven" (Matthew 18:19 EMPHASIS ADDED). There is an increase and multiplication of the anointing when two or more come together.

Jesus sent His disciples out two by two, making them a "congregation" and thereby conferring the synergy that comes with adding the corporate anointing to the individual anointing. Jesus knew this would increase their power exponentially. Wherever they went, the manifest presence of the Lord accompanied them. Jesus said,

> "For where ***two or three*** are gathered together in my name, there am I in the ***midst*** of them."
>
> —Matt. 18:20 EMPHASIS ADDED

The disciples understood the difference between the indwelling presence and the manifest presence of God. They refer to the Holy Ghost as in their midst and in their meeting. They were aware of the added presence of God and His assistance in their decision-making.

> For it seemed good to the Holy Ghost, and to us, to lay upon you no greater burden than these necessary things;
>
> —Acts 15:28

Could it be that we today make bad decisions because we have not invited the manifest presence of God into our decision-making process? Could it be that He is the missing person at the boardroom table?

He Desires to be in our Midst

It is clear that God's desire is to be in the midst of His congregation.

Isaiah is prophesying that God will be in the midst and among His people in the remnant church. Another reference to Him being among his people is the phrase, *"He will tabernacle with them."* Israel was told to build a tabernacle patterned after God's specific design given to Moses on the mount. It was to be placed in the center of the camp and the twelve tribes of Israel were to surround it. It is clear that God's desire is to be in the midst of His congregation.

Isaiah's prophecy declares that for those who long for His presence, God will be present in three ways—not just one! History records that during the Azusa Street revival, in 1906, not only did God dwell in the believers, but His manifest presence saturated the assembly. God, then, moved out from the church into the community where His presence was felt in a tangible way.

I am convinced that a great end time revival is at hand.

When the presence of the Lord filled the streets, people were drawn to God. At Azusa His manifest presence could be felt ten blocks away. The presence of God was literally sweeping through the city. Multitudes fell under the power of conviction, just walking by the building.

So influential was the Azusa Street Revival that during the San Francisco Earthquake, the Los Angeles Times felt it more important to feature the revival than the Earthquake. The front-page headline read "Wild Scenes in the Mission." The article went on to describe large flames of fire coming from the roof of the building, which got the attention of the Fire Department—unaware that it was the Fire of the Holy Spirit. Fire engines were dispatched to the mission in an attempt to extinguish the burning roof. Yet, the firefighters stood in amazement as the fire continued to burn but the roof was not consumed. Witnessing the manifest presence of God, these men were drawn to the cross of Christ.

Beloved, what accompanied the New Testament Apostles was present at Azusa Street, and is available to every generation—including ours. I am convinced that a great end time revival is at hand. It will be the greatest revival the world has ever seen.

Isaiah had his finger on the pulse of that revival when he prophesied chapter four. He declared that in the last days a greater measure of God's manifest presence would be available to the church. This is the needed power to combat the increase of sin and lawlessness in our present day culture.

The Presence of God is Revival

We see the manifest presence on the ministry of the great revivalist Charles Finney. Upon entering a community, the manifest presence of God spread from street to street. He had more than just the indwelling presence of God. He had the manifest presence of God.

One particular story tells of an encounter he had in a cotton mill. While in Utica, New York, Finney was asked to meet with the owner of the company. Though the man was not a believer, Finney felt it could be an influential opportunity to share the Gospel of Christ. As he climbed the stairs to the owner's office, he could see two women snickering at him from the factory floor. Without a message or even a spoken word, he simply starred at them. The women went from snickering to falling under the manifest presence of God. Their weeping started a chain reaction that affected everyone in the factory. Within moments the manifest presence of the Lord began to fill the entire factory. The manifest presence of God was so great that the owner shut the factory down stating, "let not our work hinder the work of God." He then asked Finney to preach the Gospel, after which all the employees were converted to Christ.

There are many other examples of the manifest presence of God falling on His people. The only requirement is a genuine desire to wholly submit to Him and invite the fullness of His presence.

8

Hungering for Jesus

Repent ye therefore, and be converted,
that your sins may be blotted out,
when the "Times of Refreshing" *shall come*
from the presence of the Lord;

—*Acts 3:19* EMPHASIS ADDED

Hungering for Jesus

Repent ye therefore, and be converted,
that your sins may be blotted out,
when the "Times of Refreshing" *shall come*
from the presence of the Lord;

—*Acts 3:19* EMPHASIS ADDED

In your hands is the wisdom and knowledge that can spark the coals of revival across this great nation. I am convinced that the manifest presence of God, which is revival, is the only thing that can restore our culture.

The presence of God can pierce the most unfavorable climates that are not conducive to revival and renewal. This is what happened when Peter stood to preach his first message. His message at Pentecost was neither eloquent nor lengthy. In fact, it was a response to accusations that they were drunk. Yet, what accompanied Peter's preaching was the manifest presence of God. During his recounting of the Gospel of Jesus Christ, the Holy Ghost descended on the people in the

Revival, is the only thing that can restore our culture.

city square and 3,000 people were saved. God manifested Himself in flaming tongues of fire. Peter worked in concert with the manifest presence of God—and impacted a community.

This is repeated throughout history in the lives of the Apostles, Jonathan Edwards, D.L. Moody, George Whitefield, the Wesley Brothers, and Charles Finney, to name a few.

A Small Spark!

You may be reading this book, thinking, "What can I do - I'm only one believer?" You might think it takes large numbers of people to create change. You would be wrong. In actuality, the majority of revivals were birthed with only a handful of individuals. It is the Gideon principle. Gideon had assembled an army that God felt was too large. He was instructed to reduce the number of soldiers so there'd be no doubt that God was the reason for the victory.

The Azusa Street revival started in a home with less than twelve people praying for revival! You might be pastoring a church thinking, "How can I compete—I do not have all the luxuries and amenities of a mega-church?" I encourage you, "that is not what is needed!" Instead, the manifest presence of God is needed.

Jesus said:

> *If* I be lifted up from the earth, *I* will draw all *men* unto me.
>
> —John 12:32 EMPHASIS ADDED

Begin to cultivate a passion for His presence and God will reveal Himself to you in ways you can not imagine.

Miracle in the Corn Fields

The Smithton Revival started in a church in the middle of nowhere. Smithton, Missouri is a town with a population of 532. The town is so small it doesn't even have a gas station. Pastor Steve Gray and his congregation prayed for God to manifest His presence and send revival. When revival broke out there were thousands of people, waiting in lines for six to eight hours—and that was without any advertising, public relations or other media. People from all over the world made their way to Smithton, led only by the Holy Spirit.

Cultivate a passion for His presence and God will reveal Himself to you

It is important to note that many of these people were in churches that had amenities, yet they were hungry for the manifest presence of God. After visiting the Smithton Church and interviewing Pastor Gray, Sid Roth commented, "Americans remain hungry for revival and are willing to travel across the country to experience His presence."

Hungry for the Presence of God

Now is the time to feed upon the bread of life. Jesus is standing at the door, knocking, longing to dine with you. He has in his hand a cloak of righteousness fitted just for you. He will remove all condemnation and doubt. He will heal all your hurts and wounds. He will establish your feet on a path of provision, protection and revival.

Now is the time to feed upon the bread of life.

> For thus saith the high and lofty One that inhabiteth eternity, whose name is Holy; I dwell in the high and holy

> place, with him also that is of a contrite and humble spirit, to revive the spirit of the humble, and to revive the heart of the contrite ones.
>
> —Isaiah 57:15

Beloved, begin to pray and ask God to manifest His presence in your church services. It is not enough to be satisfied with the indwelling presence, which only affects believers, but not the people around them. This is the way a church can begin to impact a community, region and beyond.

The Spirit of the Lord looks for groups of believers through which to manifest Himself, to pour out His Spirit in unique ways so that the world may see it and glorify Him as Lord of Lords and King of Kings.

> For the eyes of the LORD run to and fro throughout the whole earth, to shew himself strong in the behalf of them whose heart is perfect toward him.
>
> —2 Chronicles 16:9

> Repent ye therefore, and be converted, that your sins may be blotted out, ***when the times of refreshing*** shall come ***from the presence*** of the Lord;
>
> —Acts 3:19-21, EMPHASIS ADDED

Modern Christian writers have grasped the importance of acknowledging and experiencing God's presence. "Moderate success in ministry is a spiritual hazard," says Henry Blackaby. "It can make us content to live without the manifest presence of God." "Peace," writes J. Oswald Sanders, "is not the absence of trouble, but the presence of God." N. Lee Cooper, at the time president elect of the American Bar Association, said, "The only effective response to our nation's crime problem is spiritual revival." [1]

We are not left with a powerless message, but with an anointed, powerful Gospel, that has authority over the issues of life, and over every principality, power, and behavior. No matter what you've gone through, the Gospel of Jesus Christ is your refuge. The glory of the Lord can set you free and release you from the chains of hell and the bondages of your past.

> Then shall ye call upon me, and ye shall go and **pray** unto me, and I will hearken unto you
>
> —Jeremiah 29:12 EMPHASIS ADDED

> Then shall thy light break forth as the morning, and thine health shall spring forth speedily: and thy righteousness shall go before thee; the glory of the LORD shall be thy rearward
>
> —Isaiah 58:8

Isaiah reminds us of God's promise that He will create a glory that covers His remnant church. The very glory of God is going to fill every heart and cover every house. We will worship under the canopy of God's glory!

God's glory is nothing other than the manifest presence of Jesus Christ, God's Son! Jesus is the fullness of the Father's glory. Could anything be more wonderful? Could anything provide comfort and guidance in such a magnificent way? Is anything more powerful?

We will worship under the canopy of God's glory!

So it is, in the day in which we live, God is looking to pour out revival on His church. Particularly the part of the church that's allowing Christ to lay hold of them.

Beloved, we are living in serious times. This would be a good point to stop playing games with God and if you are genuinely saved, then *get serious with God*! If you are not in a good church—don't waste another minute. Find yourself a good, solid, bible-teaching church—one that does not compromise the holy standards of God. When you find such a church, join it, become active and intercede for its leadership.

Isaiah Chapter four ends with a wonderful promise that the glory of the Lord will be on His assemblies and that God will be a "covert" and a "refuge" in the midst of a chaotic world. This is *your* promise. While Isaiah paints a vivid picture of the difficulties of our time, he also assures us of the promise of ***protection, provision*** and ***revival—for every believer and church that is hungry for Jesus.***

Beloved, you can begin this awesome journey right now!

Notes

CHAPTER ONE

[1] Friends with Benefits is a common term among the youth of our day. Dateline did an entire expose on the subject. It refers to the practice of having intimate relationships with friends. There is no pretense of an ongoing relationship by either party.

[2] *Theo-phobic is a phrase the author uses to define a fear of bad or distorted theology. He is certainly not phobic about God*

[3] Some of the stats on the numerous prophecies:

> The Old Testament has **23,210** verses of scripture **6,641** of them contain prophetic information about the future. That means that over **28% of the entire Old Testament** is concerned with prophecy. The New Testament has **7,914** verses, and **1,711** of them also contain predictive information about everything from current world events to the future of the World. So out of the entire Bible's **31,124** verses, **8,352** of them are prophetic.
>
> Further **23 out of the** 27 books of the New Testament deal with the topic of the **second coming** of Jesus Christ. In the New Testament alone, **318 Bible verses – every 25th** Bible verse in the New Testament speaks of the Second Coming of our Lord.
>
> The Bible speaks of the second coming **1,845** Times. Jesus rebuke to them was that they did not understand the signs of the times, nor how God works in the affairs of men.

CHAPTER TWO

[1] Pastor Muratori preached a very thought-provoking message titled "Six Fingers and Six Toes." If you'd like to know more or order a copy of this best selling message visit his web site: www.johnmuratori.com

CHAPTER 3

[1] Anonymous, Compiled by Albert M. Wells, Jr., *Inspirations Quotations, Contemporary & Classical* (Thomas Nelson Publishers, Inc. 1988) Entry 2010

CHAPTER 5

[1] In the bible the duration of a generation is 40 years.

[2] C.S. Lewis in Present Concerns: Essays by C.S. Lewis. Christianity Today, Vol. 35, no. 2.

[3] Billy Graham in a speech at Gordon-Conwell Theological Seminary's Founder's Day (April 4, 1989). Christianity Today, Vol. 33, no. 9.

[4] Edythe Draper, *Draper's Book of Quotations for the Christian World* (Wheaton: Tyn-

dale House Publishers, Inc. 1992) Entry 9746

[5] Ibid, Entry 5759

[6] Frank Damazio, *Seasons of Revival,* Copyright 1996, Bible Temple Publishing. Portland. p.36

CHAPTER 6

[1] www.exploratorium.edu/climate/primer/index.html

(The Intergovernmental Panel on Climate Change (IPCC), a group established by the World Meteorological Organization (WMO) and the United Nations Environmental Program (UNEP) warn us about the increasing "Greenhouse Effect" stating that human activities—primarily the burning of fossil fuels, have increased the greenhouse gas content of the earth's atmosphere.)

[2] Grant R. Jeffrey, Prince of Darkness (Toronto: Frontier Research Publications, 1994), pp. 310, 311

[3] David Barton, *America. To Pray? Or Not to Pray?* Aledo, Texas 5th edition, 2nd printing 1995. P. 15

[4] Ibid

[5] Brad Macdonald, *The Ailing State of American Universities,* The Trumpet, Philadelphia, PA., July 2005

CHAPTER 7

[1] Frank Damazio, Seasons of Revival (Portland, Oregon: BT Publishing, 1996), p. 172.

CHAPTER 8

[1] *Leadership,* Vol. 16, no. 4.

~ Study Guide ~

Chapter 1

1) After reading the facts presented at the beginning of this chapter, how do you view our present culture?

2) How do you think non-believers view our culture? Why?

3) What is the prophet Isaiah referring to when he says, "in that day?"

4) In 2nd Timothy 3:15 Paul prophesies that in the "last days" men/women will have a "form of godliness, but deny the power thereof." What is he talking about?

5) If we are in "that day," what affect should it have on our lives?

Chapter 2

1) Jesus came so men/women could be saved. He also came for another specific purpose. What is it and what is its significance?

2) In the parable of the ten virgins, five are called wise—why? What are the implications of this parable for present day believers?

3) Who are the seven women of Isaiah's prophecy? Why is it important to understand what they symbolize?

4) Who is the "one man"—also referred to as "the branch?"

5) When you see the seven women as the church and the one man as Jesus Christ himself - How does it clarify your understanding of Isaiah's prophecy?

Chapter 3

1) What do the seven women want to take hold of? How does that mirror much of the church today?

2) Why is it harmful to consistently hear messages that do not challenge you to change?

3) Why did Jesus tell people what they NEEDED to hear, rather than what they WANTED to hear?

4) The prophet Amos said that in the "last days" believers would be so accustomed to eating strange bread that there would be a famine of the "Word of God." What was he referring to?

5) Why was Adam's attempt to cover his sin unsuccessful?

6) Satan can not get rid of the "robe of righteousness" so he fabricated counterfeit garments that appear to cover sin. Name some counterfeit garments that appear to cover sin, but in fact cover nothing - discuss them.

7) What qualifies a person to receive "the robe of righteousness?"

Chapter 4

1) How does our culture view Jesus? (Give some examples)

2) Why do you suppose Jesus is the only one singled out for the greatest persecution among the various faiths in our culture?

3) Why do some famous preachers limit their messages to positive, self-help subject matter?

4) Why did Jesus always tell the whole truth—no matter who heard it or how much they liked it?

5) What does it mean to be an "under-cover" Christian?

6) In Isaiah 58 we are told that God began to despise their sacrifices, services and offerings. Why was He so angry about their behavior?

7) What does the Biblical term remnant mean?

8) What will the characteristics of the true "last days" church be?

Chapter 5

1) One of the attributes of God is faithfulness. Why is that important in the times in which we live?

2) God protected the nation of Israel from the armies of Egypt. It was not important for them to know HOW He would deliver them; rather it was important that they trusted Him to deliver them. How does that relate to the challenge before us today?

3) The term "backslidden" is most often used in reference to an individual. In this chapter it is used to refer to the church. How does it fit today's church?

4) Christianity has been so watered down that there is, in some facets of the church, no distinct difference between the church and secular society. What does that say about the condition of the church today?

5) What effect did President Clinton's moral failure have on our society as a whole?

6) When a culture tolerates and even justifies sin, decay is inevitable. When revival comes, sin will be revealed for what it is. How can you get prepared now?

Chapter 6

1) In this chapter the following statement is made, "In my opinion, ninety-nine percent of people's problems are not the result of God's judgment; rather they are the result of people making bad decisions." How do you feel about that?

2) What part does mankind play in the destruction of the balance God has created in nature?

3) What is the "butterfly effect?"

4) The acknowledgement of God is being completely removed from our society—causing a significant "*butterfly effect.*" What are some results of that butterfly effect?

5) What has happened to our school systems since prayer was removed from the classroom?

6) How has the process of higher education (colleges and universities) degenerated over the last three to four decades?

7) When God is asked to leave a society, what happens to some of the inherent protection that comes with His presence? What impact can that have?

Chapter 7

1) What characteristics dominate a properly functioning church?

2) What was it that empowered the disciples in the early church to turn a region upside down, though they had no special tools or modern day aids?

3) What are the three aspects of the "presence" of God?

4) Define the three aspects of the presence of the Lord.

5) In our day most believers are aware of the "indwelling" presence of God but they are unaware or uninformed about the "omnipresence" and the "manifest presence" of God. Why is that a problem?

6) What's wrong with saying, "I don't need to go to church. God dwells in me already?" (Reference the GE example for clarification)

7) How was the "manifest presence" of God influential in the Azusa Street Revival?

Chapter 8

1) Why is the "manifest presence" of God the only thing that can restore our culture?

2) Why do you think most revivals began with a small amount of praying people?

3) Henry Blackaby states that, "moderate success in ministry is a spiritual hazard." Why is that?

4) Isaiah speaks of the protection of the Lord for the Remnant Church. How will that protection manifest itself?

5) Isaiah chapter four ends with a wonderful promise. What is it and why is it important to every passionate believer?

About the Author

John Muratori is a dynamic and progressive speaker with a unique message that crosses denominational and cultural barriers. Known for Vision Casting, Strategic Planning and Wealth Building, John has advised many organizations and governmental agencies including the *"Dept. of Homeland Security" and "Dept. of Mental Health."* His counsel is widely sought after by CEO's, entrepreneurs, millionaires and ministers.

John is the Executive Director of Turning Point Christian Center, a nationally renowned residential substance abuse rehabilitation program, with one of the highest success rates in the country. John's proven techniques for reversing the destructive behavioral patterns linked to addiction have put TPCC on the forefront of compassion ministry.

He is the General Overseer of ***Bethel Fellowship***, a global network of churches and ministries. John is the Founder of ***Vanguard Ministry Training School***, a fully accredited Bible school.

John is an author and sought after conference speaker. He reaches people across the country and the world with his insights on leadership, organizational excellence and program development. He is the author of several books, including *"Rich Church, Poor Church."*

John Muratori is a graduate of Antioch University International in Dallas, Texas and is currently working on his Ph.D from CLU in Buffalo, New York. John is the Senior Pastor of Calvary Life Christian Center in Cheshire, Connecticut, and a member of ICA, founded by Dr. C. Peter Wagner. With strong leadership combined with two decades of ministerial experience, John is developing the next generation of leaders. He and his wife Carmela live with their two sons in Wolcott, CT.

~New Book Release~

Rich Church Poor Church

---

by John Louis Muratori

Schedule A Seminar

The Rich Church Seminar will expand the impact and influence of local churches and equip both individuals and organizations with stewardship principles for financial independence.

This power-packed seminar offers fresh, Biblical revelation on wealth and finances and their relationship to God's people. Proper application of the principles given can change your life completely!

The ***Rich Church Seminar*** provides each attendee with a foundational understanding on creating wealth. Each event imparts God's concepts on:

- ***The Twelve Pillars of Building Wealth***
- ***Overcoming a Poverty Mentality***
- ***Why The Wicked Prosper***
- ***Pivotal Organizational Transitions***
- ***Creative Wealth and Income Strategies***

College and Career Workshop

Because of our commitment to the next generation, we have developed a workshop specifically for senior high and college students. This workshop will equip young people with practical wealth strategies as they chart the course for their lives. ***This workshop is offered at a 25% discount.***

For more information or to schedule a seminar at your church or organization please e-mail: info@richchurch.net

"It is my passion to create millions of dollars through local churches to transform communities across this nation."

—John L. Muratori

Additional Resources from John Muratori

MVP:
Mission, Vision and Purpose

Do you feel lost and without real direction in your life?

You are not alone. Many people never lay hold of a mission for their lives. Without such a mission—mediocrity and aimlessness are most often the only possible destination.

This should not be so. God has pre-destined and called every believer to achieve their **greatest potential and personal impact**. Within you lie the God-given abilities to accomplish that awesome destiny.

In this series John Muratori will answer the following questions:

- "Why am I here?"
- "What am I supposed to be doing?"
- "What does my future destination look like?"

This series will empower and teach you how to live with a Mission, Vision and Purpose. It will be a life characterized by God's very best for you.

Overcoming Strife

The statistics are in.
Not even the church is immune to divorce!

The divorce epidemic is fueled by conflict and unbridled strife. Unchecked, it will single-handedly destroy an individual and all his/her relationships.

Our nation's young people are being defined as rebellious, confused and disrespectful. Why? Because they are not being taught how to have healthy relationships and how to handle strife.

Overcoming Strife will give you the tools necessary to not only contend with strife but to overcome it. It will help you restore peace to your relationships and to your life. You will never handle conflict the same old way again!

Song of Solomon

Learn the keys to experiencing successful relationships found in the most misunderstood book in the Bible.

This powerful series guides you through the Art of:

- Attraction
- Dating
- Courtship
- Conflict

Whether you are single, married or divorced,
Song of Solomon will transform your relationships!

Life On The Edge

Are you at a crossroads?

One way or another, we all get to the edge of ourselves-to a defining moment when we either fall out of God's divine plan or we cling to Him and He lifts us to an exciting, new level of faith.

Life on the Edge will help you to come away from the edge of giving up on your dreams and visions, and will bring you to the edge of personal revival and breakthrough.

Topics Covered:

- Overcoming Spiritual Depletion
- Overcoming The Past
- Breaking The Strongholds That Bind Us
- The Power of Decisions
- The Great Identity Crisis
- The Power Of Our Beliefs
- The Breakthrough Toolbox

And More!

Exposé On Temptation

Do you find yourself falling into the same self-destructive traps again and again?

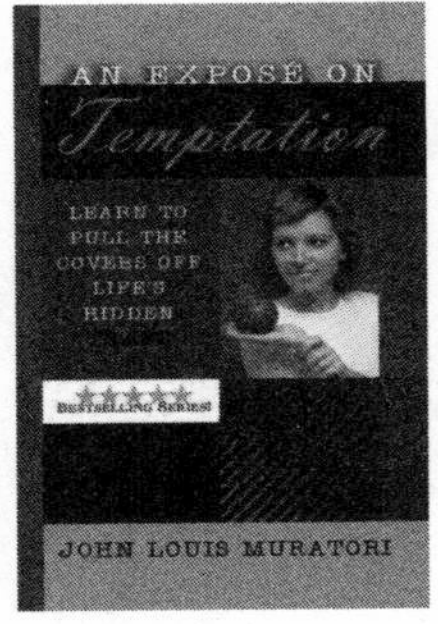

Many believers feel caught in vicious cycles of habitual sin. Although they try to live fruitful lives, their failures and shortcomings produce frustration, disappointment and helplessness.

In this powerful series, John Muratori will help you:

- Identify the strategies set up to ensnare you
- Expose the multiple methods the enemy uses to trick mankind
- Uncover the five components of a satanic trap

By walking in the principles laid out in this series you will live a *transformed* life—free from bondage and filled with *freedom.*

YOU CAN FIND THESE AND MANY OTHER POWERFUL MESSAGES ONLINE BY VISITING WWW.JOHNMURATORI.COM.

John Muratori Ministries
PO Box 1216, Cheshire, CT 06410

(203) 272-1701

Additional Resources

from Nick Gugliotti

About Nick's Upcoming Release

Several years ago, my life took a sudden and unexpected turn. I went from executive on the rise, to unemployed and battling a serious illness. The illness, although potentially terminal, has not killed me. The heart-wrenching, soul-challenging battle to re-define myself almost did. It's the story I tell in "***I Had Other Plans, Lord***". If you have experienced any sudden and dramatic life-change, I believe this book can help. I understand what you are going through and I respect you enough to tell the whole truth. I will not give you false hope. I will share with you the real hope that can never be shaken. It's my heartfelt prayer that the pieces of your healing can be found in "***I Had Other Plans, Lord.***"

What others are saying

"This book is for everyone whose life story has encountered a plot twist – a critical moment that changes everything. Read Nick's story and be inspired!"

—Les Parrott, Ph.D.
Seattle Pacific University
Founder of The Center For Relationship Development
Author of "***Shoulda, Coulda, Woulda*" *and bestseller* "*Saving Your Marriage Before It Starts*".**

If your heart is injured, your life feeling turned upside down, "***I Had Other Plans, Lord***" offers the guidance and encouragement you will need to heal, hope, and turn things right-side up again. In this book filled with biblical wisdom and inspiring stories about courageous survivors, Nick Gugliotti shares how he overcame a serious setback in his life and learned to trust God for wholeness. The clearly taught principals and Reader's Guide for Personal Reflection make this book ideal for group study.

—Alec Hill
President and CEO of InterVarsity Christian Fellowship/USA
Author of ***Just Business***

About Nick Gugliotti

Nick Gugliotti spent over two decades in the communications industry. He founded two successful advertising/marketing companies. He has served in numerous leadership capacities such as Elder, Associate Pastor, and Bible teacher. He has a Masters Degree in Communications from Fairfield University and has been recognized by the American Association of Christian Counselors. He has been writing professionally for over twenty years—with credits in print, radio and TV. Nick's next book—***I Had Other Plans, Lord***, will be released in 2006. Information and excerpts from the book, along with other resources can be found @ Nick Gugliotti www.nickgugliotti.com.